THE BASICS OF NUCLEAR PHYSICS

CORE CONCEPTS

THE BASICS OF NUCLEAR PHYSICS

CHRISTOPHER COOPER

ROSEN PUBLISHING

Published in 2025 by The Rosen Publishing Group, Inc.
2544 Clinton Street, Buffalo, NY 14224

First edition published 2015. Second edition 2025.

Editor: Ashley Brown
Design manager: Keith Davis
Picture manager: Sophie Mortimer

Cataloging-in-Publication Data

Names: Cooper, Christopher, 1944-.
Title: The basics of nuclear physics / Christopher Cooper.
Description: Second edition. | Buffalo, NY : Rosen Young Adult, 2025. | Series: Core concepts | Audience: Grade 7-12. | Includes glossary and index.
Identifiers: ISBN 9781499478136 (pbk.) | ISBN 9781499478143 (library bound) | ISBN 9781499478150 (ebook)
Subjects: LCSH: Nuclear physics--Juvenile literature.
Classification: LCC QC778.5 C663 2025 | DDC 539.7--dc23

Manufactured in the United States of America

CPSIA Compliance Information: Batch #CW25RYA. For further information, contact Rosen Publishing, New York, New York, at 1-800-237-9932.

CONTENTS

CHAPTER 1

Exploring the Atom

All matter is made up of tiny particles called atoms. In turn, atoms are themselves made up of even smaller particles: protons, neutrons, and electrons. The properties of matter depend on the structure of the atom.

↑ A massive star explodes as a supernova, scattering the atoms "cooked" in its core. They may become the building materials of new stars and their planets.

All the matter around us is made up from atoms—particles so small that about 100 million atoms can span one fingernail. There are about 5,000 trillion trillion atoms in your body. Yet in 1897 the English physicist J. J. Thomson found that atoms contain even smaller particles, later called electrons.

Electrons have negative electric charge. There also has to be positive charge in the atom to balance these negative charges. Thomson suggested that the electrons were embedded in a globe of positive electricity, like raisins in a plum pudding. But then Ernest Rutherford, a New Zealander, found that the atom's positive charge, and most of its mass, lies at its center in a core called the nucleus (plural nuclei). The atom is held together by the electrical attraction of the positive nucleus for the negative electrons.

↑ Everything on Earth, from a giant African elephant to the tiniest microscopic organism, is made up of atoms.

EARLY MODELS OF THE ATOM

Early theorists, such as John Dalton, regarded the atom as having no structure. J. J. Thomson found that it contained negatively charged electrons.

Rutherford showed that the balancing positive charge was concentrated in a nucleus, and Niels Bohr calculated the sizes of the electrons' orbits.

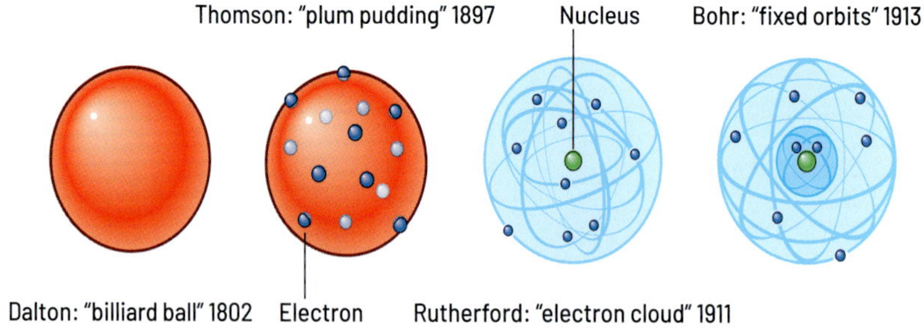

BUILDING THE ELEMENTS

The simplest atomic nucleus is that of hydrogen, a single positively charged proton. Atoms of other elements contain more protons, with uncharged neutrons to hold them together.

The number of protons is called the atomic number, shown below in brackets. Ordinarily the protons' positive charge is balanced by an equal number of electrons.

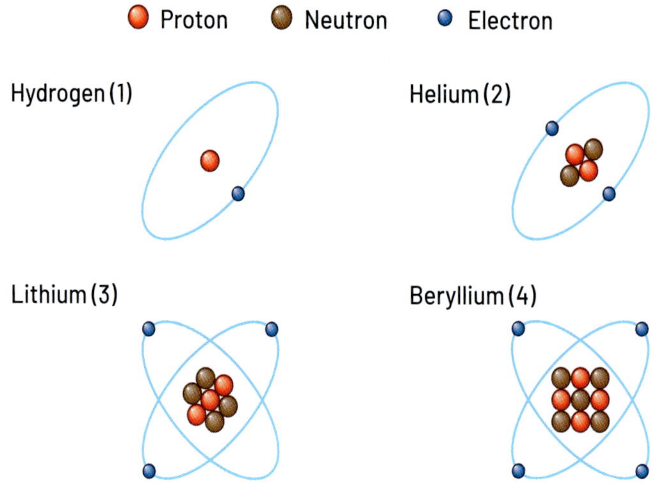

NIELS BOHR

Niels Bohr was involved in the creation of the European Organization for Nuclear Research, or CERN, in 1954.

The Danish physicist Niels Bohr, born in 1885, provided the first clues to the structure of the atom. He assumed the electrons circled the nucleus like planets orbiting the Sun. A major problem was that, according to the theory then existing, whirling electrons should radiate all their energy in a burst of electromagnetic radiation and fall into the nucleus in a fraction of a second. Bohr could not explain why this did not happen, but went ahead and assumed the electrons stayed in fixed orbits. He was able to calculate their size and energy for the simplest atom, hydrogen. Bohr received the Nobel Prize in Physics in 1922. He played a large part in developing quantum theory, which deals with the physics of the very small, and which has replaced his simple model of the atom with a more complicated one.

Protons and Neutrons

Later experimenters found that the nucleus is itself made up of particles, or nucleons. They are of two types. One is the proton, which has an electric charge equal but opposite to that of the electron. The mass of the proton is nearly 2,000 times as great as that of the electron. The other type of nucleon is electrically neutral (uncharged) and so is called the neutron. Its mass is approximately equal to that of the proton.

Protons, neutrons, and electrons were built up into atoms in the fireball of the Big Bang, 15 billion or so years ago. But only the simplest and lightest atoms were formed then. Since then, light atoms have been welded together in the centers of stars to form more complex atoms. That is where the carbon, oxygen, nitrogen, and other atoms in your body originated. If a star explodes as a supernova, these and heavier atoms are spread through interstellar space.

CHAPTER 2

The Nucleus of the Atom

All the atoms of a particular element have the same number of protons in their nucleus. The number of neutrons may vary, however. Atoms with the same number of protons but different numbers of neutrons are called isotopes. Some isotopes are stable; others are unstable.

There are about 90 kinds of naturally occurring, chemically different atoms on Earth. They behave very differently in chemical reactions—some react strongly; some react scarcely at all. All these differences are a result of the activity

Most water on Earth is light water, consisting of ordinary hydrogen combined with oxygen. A tiny fraction, only one part in 6,000, is heavy water, in which the hydrogen is replaced by deuterium.

NAMING ISOTOPES

The two rare isotopes of hydrogen are deuterium and tritium. They have one or two neutrons, respectively. Most isotopes, such as the two carbon isotopes shown here, have no special name. They are identified by the name of the element combined with the mass number, which is the number of protons and neutrons in the nucleus.

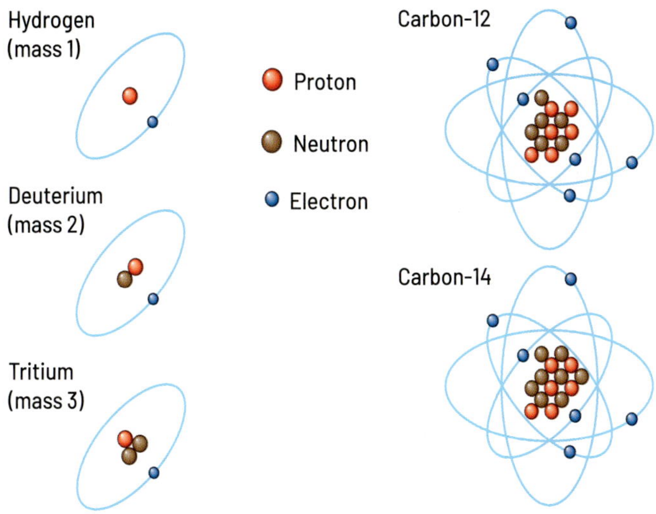

of electrons in the outer parts of the atoms. Atoms join and separate as they gain, lose, or share electrons. The behavior of the atoms depends on the number of electrons in the atoms that are reacting, and that depends on the atom's nucleus.

In ordinary conditions the number of electrons in an atom equals the number of protons in the nucleus, so that the atom is uncharged overall. This number is called the atomic number, and it is what defines an element. Fluorine has nine electrons and it has that number because there are nine protons in its nucleus. But it has a strong tendency to gain an extra electron because 10 electrons make a very stable system—that is, one that is not easily changed. So fluorine reacts strongly with other atoms from which it can gain an electron. It reacts especially strongly with sodium, which has 11 electrons, and which "tries" to shed one of them to leave just 10 electrons. A sodium and a fluorine atom join together, and an electron is transferred from the sodium to the fluorine, giving out energy in the form of heat.

But two atoms can have the same atomic number and yet differ in important ways. Although they have the same number of protons in the nucleus and are therefore

MASS SPECTROGRAPH

The collimating slits let through a narrow beam of ions. The combination of the electric field and the magnetic field causes ions of different mass to move in curves of different radii, striking the photographic plate at different positions.

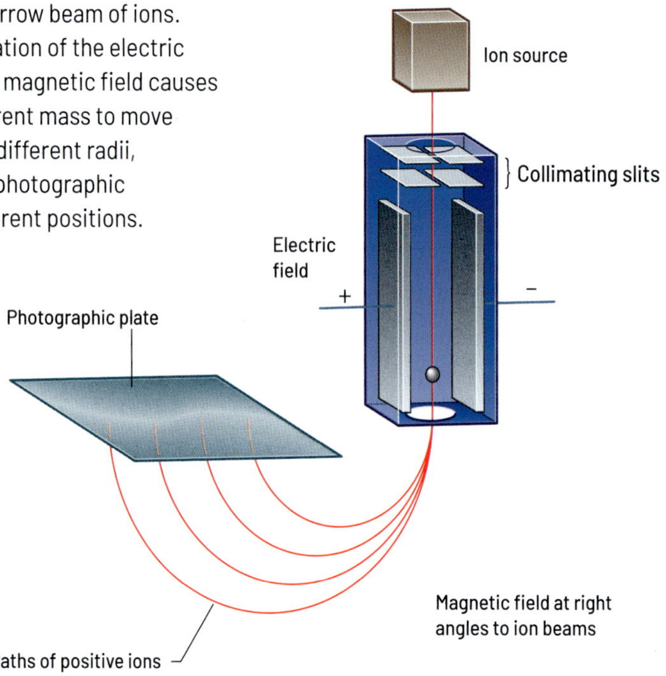

chemically identical, they can have different numbers of neutrons. Ordinary hydrogen has a nucleus consisting of one proton and no neutrons. A rarer form has one proton joined to one neutron in the nucleus and is called deuterium. A still rarer form has one proton and two neutrons in the nucleus, and is called tritium.

Discovering Isotopes

These different forms of an element are called isotopes of that element. They were first discovered by J. J. Thomson, discoverer of the electron, who found two varieties of the gas neon. His student Francis Aston studied isotopes thoroughly when he made very accurate measurements of the masses of atoms from 1919 onward. Aston formed beams of fast-moving ions. Ions are atoms that have lost or gained one or more electrons to form electrically charged particles. They can be accelerated by passing them through an electric field. Magnetic fields have the effect of bending the paths of electrically charged particles. Aston passed his ion beams through both electric and

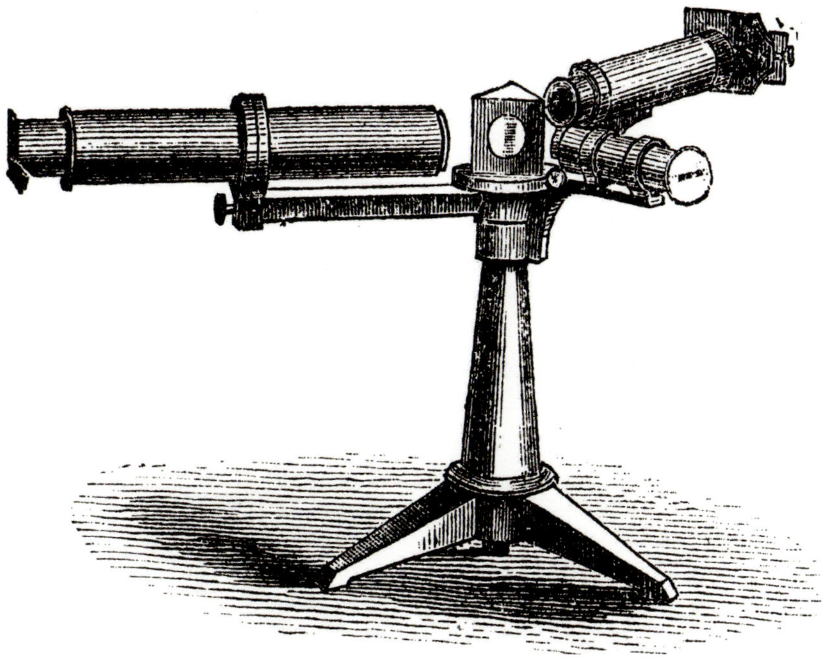

Mass spectrographs are essential to the work of modern chemical laboratories. Today's instruments work on the same basic principles as the first one built in 1919. But they are now so sensitive they can detect differences in relative atomic mass as small as one part in 100,000.

magnetic fields, and was able to separate them into beams depending on the charge and mass of the ions. He called his device a mass spectrometer because it spread out the beams of ions in much the same way as an optical spectrometer spreads out a beam of light. Closely related devices are called mass spectroscopes and mass spectrographs. Such experiments show that, for example, chlorine atoms are of two main types. Approximately three-fourths have a mass 35 times that of the hydrogen atom; the other fourth have a mass 37 times that of the hydrogen atom. This explained why chemists had already found that the mass of the chlorine atom is 35 to 45 times that of hydrogen: they had been measuring an average. The mass of an atom is expressed as its relative atomic mass, or r.a.m. (this used to be called its atomic weight). The r.a.m. of the most common isotope of carbon, with six protons and six neutrons, is defined to be exactly equal to 12; on this scale the r.a.m. of hydrogen is 1.008.

Seeking Stability

There must be at least as many neutrons as protons to make a stable nucleus—that is, one that will last unchanged. If there are too

FRANCIS ASTON

Francis Aston gained the first clue to the existence of isotopes when working with J. J. Thomson at Cambridge University in 1913, but further study was interrupted by World War I (1914–1918). In 1919 Aston built a much improved version of the equipment he had previously used. The device revealed that atoms that were chemically identical could have slightly different masses. Nearly every element studied was found to have several isotopes. Aston announced the whole-number rule, which states that the masses of isotopes are whole-number multiples of the mass of the hydrogen atom. He also discovered the rule of odd and even: Elements of odd-numbered relative atomic mass (r.a.m.) usually have isotopes of odd-numbered r.a.m., and those of even r.a.m. usually have isotopes of even r.a.m. Aston spent the rest of his career building ever more accurate mass spectrometers.

↑ Francis William Aston won the Nobel Prize in Chemistry in 1922 for his precision work in measuring the masses of atoms.

few or too many neutrons, the nucleus will disintegrate, or break down. It will do this by giving out particles or breaking in two to form other nuclei. That can happen repeatedly until stable nuclei are formed. The breaking down of a nucleus, transforming it into others, is called radioactivity. (Another type of radioactivity involves just giving out energy in the form of radiation, without changing the identity of the nucleus.) In nuclei of low atomic number there can be stable nuclei with equal numbers of neutrons and protons, as in the cases of carbon (atomic number 6), oxygen (atomic number 8), and calcium (atomic number 20). But because all protons have positive electrical charge, they tend to repel one another.

As a result, heavier nuclei need extra neutrons to hold the nucleus together against the force of repulsion between the many protons. The most stable isotope of uranium (atomic number 92) has 146 neutrons, but even so is weakly radioactive.

Uranium was first discovered in the mineral pitchblende, or uraninite, by Martin Heinrich Kleproth in 1789.

CHAPTER 3

Separating Isotopes

After scientists discovered the existence of isotopes, they wanted to separate them so they could be studied. This was a difficult process, but the race to build the first nuclear bomb during World War II provided the solution. Now the technology has many peaceful uses, such as in medical diagnosis, biological studies, and in industry.

Once scientists had discovered isotopes, they started work to separate them. That was not easy, because the isotopes of an element are chemically identical and so

↓ The city of Oak Ridge, Tennessee, developed from the engineering plant set up in 1942 to produce uranium-235 for the nuclear bomb project.

TWO METHODS OF SEPARATION

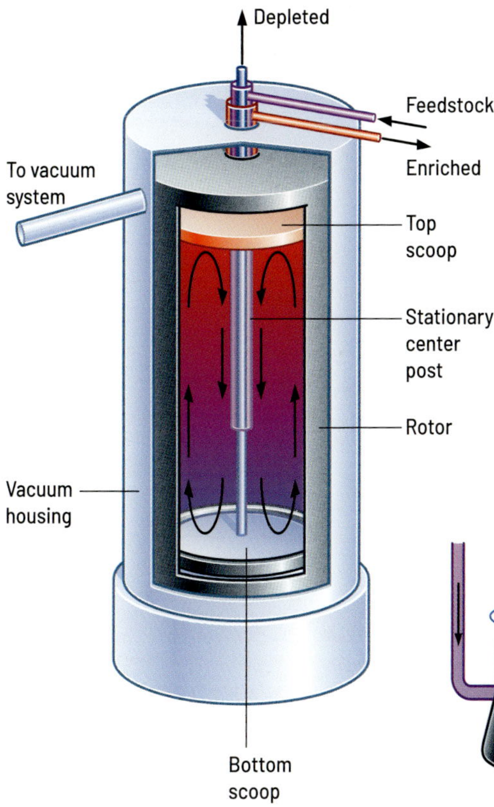

Centrifugal separation

A centrifugal separation unit receives a mixture of gaseous isotopes as "feedstock" and returns one stream of gas that is enriched in the lighter isotope and another that is depleted.

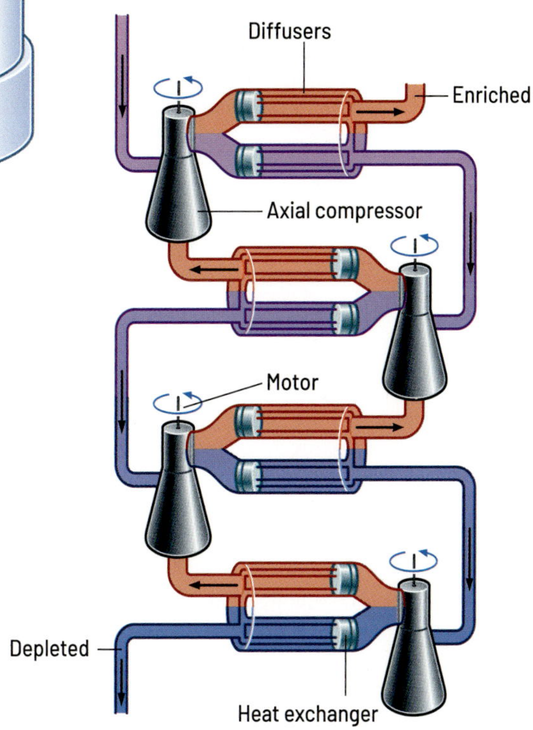

Gas-diffusion separation

At each stage of a gas-diffusion separation plant the depleted part of the output is sent on, while the enriched part is passed back to an earlier stage.

Harold Urey, far left, was appointed to the S-1 Executive Committee. This later became the Manhattan Project, a research and development program to produce the first nuclear weapons.

are affected in exactly the same way by any given chemical process. The principle behind the mass spectrograph was developed for large-scale processes. Substances with a mixture of isotopes are ionized, and a beam of the ions is passed through electric and magnetic fields. The beam splits up because the ions that have less mass are more readily deflected.

The first person to succeed in separating isotopes on a large scale was the American chemist Harold Urey. In 1932 he successfully separated the rare isotopes of hydrogen, called deuterium and tritium, from the common isotope. He did this by the electrolysis of water—that is, by breaking down water into hydrogen and oxygen by passing an electric current through it. The hydrogen that is released bubbles off, but the heavier isotopes do so more slowly. The water left behind is slightly enriched in the rare isotopes.

Two Deadly Bombs

During World War II the United States and its Allies launched a huge effort to build the first nuclear bombs. Two types of bomb were built. One required uranium-235, a rare isotope of uranium. It contains 92 protons and 143 neutrons in the nucleus. It had to be separated from the common isotope, uranium-238, in which the nucleus contains 146 neutrons.

Uranium was combined with fluorine to make the gas uranium hexafluoride. It was allowed to diffuse through a porous membrane. The uranium-235 moved slightly faster, so the gas that emerged was slightly enriched. The gas was put through the same process thousands of times, gradually increasing the proportion of uranium-235. Then electromagnetic separation was used for the final enrichment.

Similar processes were needed to produce the other type of nuclear bomb. This used the artificial element plutonium, which first had to be separated from uranium.

Another technique is centrifugal separation. A gaseous mixture of isotopes is passed into a fast-spinning chamber. The heavier isotopes are thrown outward to the edge of the rotating chamber slightly more strongly than are the lighter isotopes, and so there is partial separation. Streams of gas are collected from the center and the edge of the centrifuge by two "scoops." (See the illustrations on page 17.)

↑ These gas centrifuges in use in the 1980s are each about 40 feet (12 m) tall. Modern centrifuges are about 15 feet (4 m) tall.

CHAPTER 4

Exploring Radiation

Some isotopes change over time because of changes in the nucleus of their atoms. Most atoms are stable, but some can change from one kind to another. When they do this, they usually give out radiation in a process called radioactivity. Radiation is silent, invisible, and can be extremely dangerous.

GEIGER COUNTER

The Geiger counter can detect individual particles. A high voltage is applied between a tube-shaped cathode (a negative terminal) and the anode (a positive terminal), which takes the form of a wire running along the center of the cathode. When a charged particle passes through the tube, it knocks electrons out of atoms of gas in the tube. The positively charged ions formed move slowly, but the negatively charged electrons move rapidly toward the central anode. They knock more electrons out of atoms, so that a cascade of electrons reaches the anode. The electrons then flow along the external wires in the form of an electric current, creating a click in the loudspeaker.

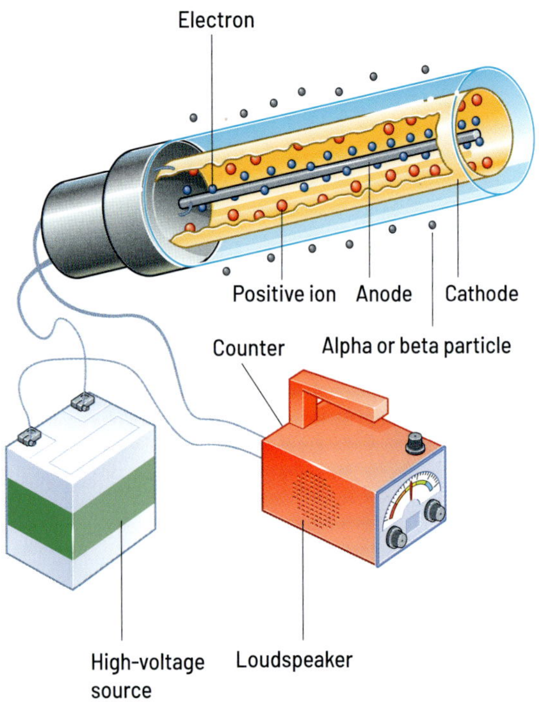

Most of the atoms around us are stable—they do not change. Most are much older than the solar system, which was formed about 5 billion years ago. But some isotopes change over time because of changes in the nucleus of their atoms. Nucleons—protons and neutrons, the particles that make up the nucleus—change into other nucleons, and often particles are expelled from the nucleus altogether. At the same time, electromagnetic radiation such as gamma rays may be given out. Radioactivity is what scientists call this type of breakdown of atoms with the emission of particles and radiation.

The radiation given out can be detected in various ways. For example, it can fog a photographic film (the kind used in old-fashioned cameras). That is how Henri Becquerel, a French physicist, discovered radioactivity in 1896. By chance he left film, wrapped in paper to keep out the light, in a desk drawer with a uranium-containing material. When he developed the film he saw that it was

↑ A Geiger counter is portable and sturdy. The rate at which it clicks and the indication on the dial give a rough measure of the intensity of any radioactivity that is present.

darkened. He investigated and found that uranium gave out a previously unknown kind of radiation capable of penetrating the paper and fogging the film.

Electronic instruments can also detect radioactivity. And living bodies can be affected. Excessive levels of radioactivity cause burning, nausea, and illness called radiation sickness. Yet carefully controlled doses of such radiation can be useful and are used in medicine to treat tumors.

Low levels of natural radioactivity surround us permanently. They originate from radioactive elements in rocks, particularly in "hard rock" areas based on granite and other igneous rocks. Natural radiation also comes from cosmic rays, which bombard Earth from space all the time.

Alpha, Beta, Gamma

Scientists in the early 20th century did not know whether radioactivity consisted of particles or of waves. But then three kinds of radiation were identified and given the names alpha, beta, and gamma radiation, after the first three letters of the Greek alphabet. Alpha radiation could be blocked merely by a piece of paper. Its path was slightly bent in a magnetic field, in a direction that showed it was made of

THREE TYPES OF RADIOACTIVITY

A sheet of paper can stop alpha particles (helium nuclei), while an aluminum sheet 1/5 inch (5 mm) thick can stop beta particles (fast-moving electrons). But lead 4/5 inch (2 cm) thick is needed to stop gamma rays (high-energy electromagnetic radiation).

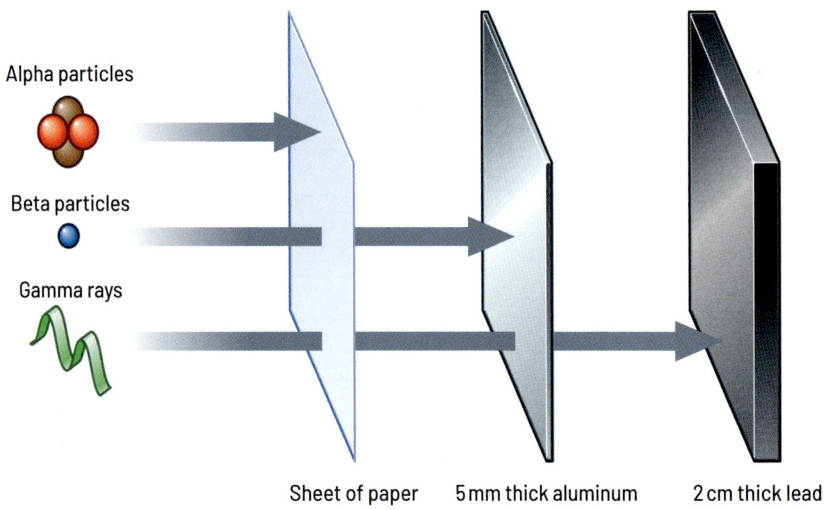

SEPARATING RADIATIONS

Applying a magnetic field shows that three kinds of radiation are given out by radioactive substances. Alpha radiation is slightly deflected, showing that it consists of positively charged particles of relatively high mass. Beta radiation is strongly deflected in the opposite direction, showing that it consists of much lighter particles with a negative charge. A third component, gamma radiation, is unaffected by the magnetic field because it consists of electromagnetic radiation.

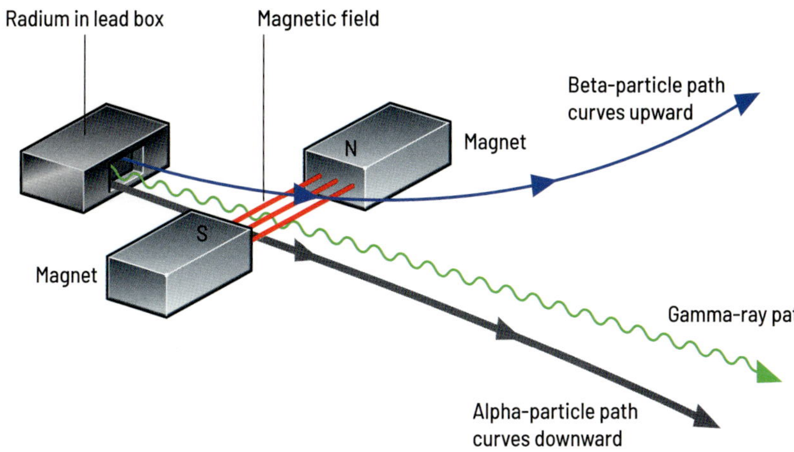

positively charged particles. Beta radiation was bent the opposite way, but much more strongly, showing that it consisted of extremely light, negatively charged particles. But gamma rays could not be bent by any electric or magnetic fields. They are electromagnetic radiation, like X-rays, but with shorter wavelengths and higher energy. Later experimenters showed that alpha particles are nuclei of helium atoms, being "packages" of two protons bound to two neutrons. Beta particles are simply electrons created by processes that take place within the nucleus.

Changes in Nuclei

Radioactivity is caused by changes in nuclei. The breakdown of an atom to form a new one is called radioactive decay. The changes come about because there is an imbalance between the numbers of protons and neutrons in the nucleus. Inside the nucleus protons and neutrons can change into one another. If there are too many neutrons, one can turn into a proton. At the same time an electron is created, so that the total charge is the same as it was before the change. (The total amount of electric charge cannot be changed in any process.)

The electron is ejected as a fast-moving beta particle, while the proton remains behind as part of the new nucleus.

An example of this process is the radioactive decay of a radioisotope (a radioactive isotope) of carbon, carbon-14. Its nucleus contains six protons and eight neutrons. After the electron has been ejected, there are seven protons and seven neutrons. This is a nucleus of nitrogen, a gas that makes up four-fifths of air.

An example of alpha decay is the decay of the common isotope of uranium, uranium-238. It is only weakly radioactive, but occasionally it gives out an alpha particle. The alpha particle takes away two units of positive charge and four mass units. The nucleus that is left behind has a mass number that is lower by four and an atomic number that is lower by two. This is a nucleus of thorium-234, which is highly radioactive.

SOURCE OF RADIOACTIVITY

In radioactivity, the radiations come from the heart of the atom. An alpha particle consists of two protons joined to two neutrons. A beta particle is an electron created by nuclear processes. Gamma rays are very short-wavelength, high-energy electromagnetic radiation.

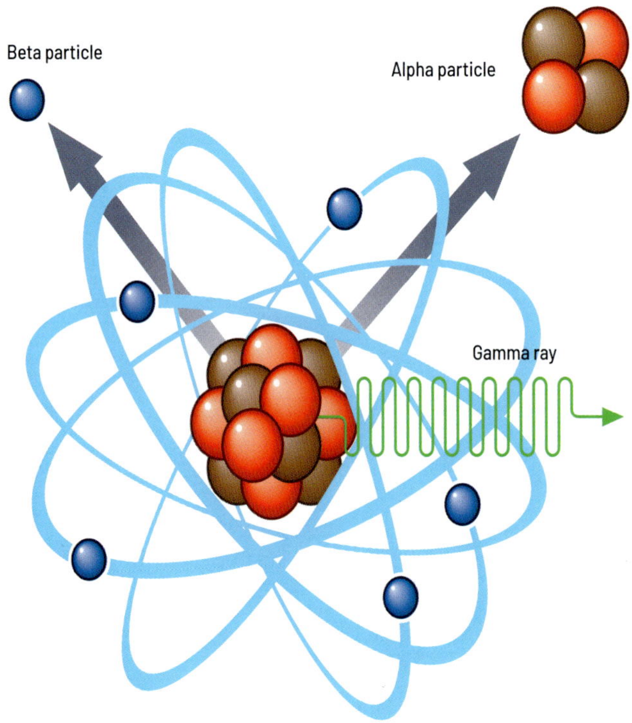

MARIE CURIE

Marie Curie pioneered the study of radioactivity, discovered new elements, and promoted radiation therapy. She was born Maria Sklodowska in Poland in 1867, but studied and worked in France.

In 1898 she discovered that the uranium mineral pitchblende gave off surprisingly strong radiation of the kind recently discovered by Henri Becquerel. With her husband, Pierre Curie, she worked to discover what unknown element in pitchblende might be responsible. She first discovered a new element that she called "polonium" after her native Poland. Then she discovered an even more strongly radioactive element, which she called "radium." The Curies shared the 1903 Nobel Prize in Physics with Becquerel. Three years later Pierre Curie was killed in an accident. In 1911 Marie Curie won the Nobel Prize in Chemistry.

She died in 1934 of a blood disease probably brought on by her years of work with radioactivity.

↑ Marie Curie was the first woman to win a Nobel Prize and the only person to win in two different sciences, physics and chemistry.

Particles and Antiparticles

Other kinds of particles can be given out in radioactivity. Orbital electrons can be ejected from the atom. Or positrons may be emitted from the nucleus. They are "antielectrons," identical in mass to electrons, but with an equal positive charge. (Every subatomic particle has a mirror-image antiparticle with opposite properties. Even the neutron has an antineutron; although they both have zero electric charge, they have opposite magnetic properties.) A positron given out in radioactive decay soon collides with an electron, and the two particles disappear completely, giving out a flash of radiation.

In the medical imaging technique called positron emission tomography (PET) a radioisotope is injected into the body. The isotope is only weakly radioactive, so there is no risk to the patient. It gives out positrons, which are annihilated in collisions with electrons, creating flashes of light that can be detected and turned into an image showing the shape of the organs in which the radioisotope has gathered.

Neutron Radiation

Some radioactive nuclei give out neutrons. Nuclear reactors, which generate energy in nuclear power stations, produce neutrons in large numbers. Neutrons are an extremely penetrating form of radiation because they are electrically neutral. Charged particles, by contrast, are easily stopped by matter because they interact with the electrons in the atoms of the matter, tending to knock them out of their atoms and losing energy in the process. Uncharged particles slip through matter easily.

However, neutrons outside the nucleus themselves actually decay. A neutron turns into a proton and an electron, which can be very damaging to living tissues. (A harmless third particle, called an antineutrino, and a flash of radiation are also emitted.)

BUBBLE CHAMBER

Liquid hydrogen is kept just below its boiling point in a radiation-shielded chamber. Lowering the piston releases pressure, and the liquid hydrogen starts boiling along the trail of ionization left by the incoming particles.

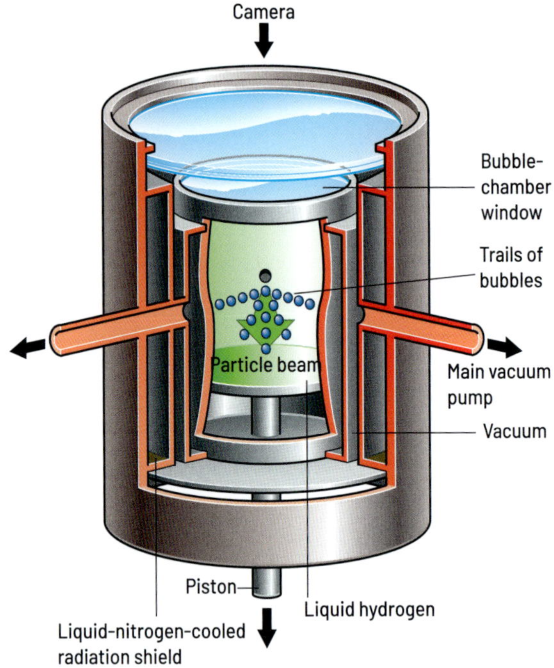

Cloud and Bubble Chambers

The detection of subatomic particles was revolutionized by the invention of the cloud chamber, the first of which was built by the British physicist C. T. R. Wilson in 1911. It was able not only to detect charged particles but to show their tracks.

It consisted of a small chamber containing dust-free air and water vapor. The chamber was suddenly expanded, causing the

BACKGROUND RADIATION

We are constantly bombarded by natural radioactivity from our surroundings. Radon gas is given off by rocks and in some areas can become a danger if it accumulates in basements. Radioactive elements absorbed by plants and animals turn up in the food we eat, and there is a constant stream of cosmic rays from outer space.

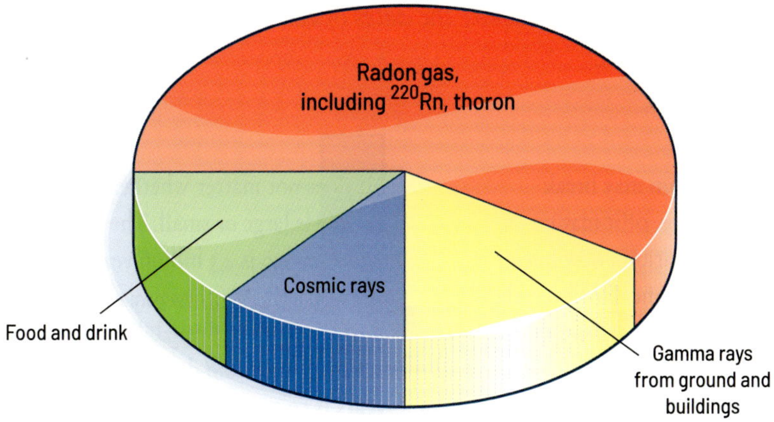

temperature of the air to drop quickly. The water vapor condensed into droplets of water on any trail of ions left by a charged particle traveling through the chamber. Uncharged particles did not form trails. These trails, resembling the condensation trails of high-flying airplanes, could be photographed.

The bubble chamber uses liquid hydrogen rather than air saturated with water vapor, and the trails consist of bubbles of boiling hydrogen, rather than droplets of water. More reactions occur in the liquid hydrogen, which is denser than the air of the cloud chamber, and the bubble chamber can provide pictures faster than the cloud chamber can. Bubble chambers have now almost completely replaced cloud chambers.

Everyday Radiation

Measurements of radioactivity show that it is around us all the time at low levels. Elements such as uranium and thorium have been present in rocks since Earth was formed. They give off a radioactive gas, radon, which in certain areas can accumulate in the basements of houses. There is a tiny fraction of radioactive carbon-14 among the ordinary carbon-12 found in the air and in the tissues of all living things. In addition to these natural sources there is very slight radioactivity from artificial sources. Some is left over from nuclear weapons testing of the past, which is now banned above ground. And there have also been some accidental releases from nuclear power plants.

EXAMPLES OF RADIOACTIVE DECAY

Atomic number and mass number change as a result of radioactive decay, except in the case of gamma radiation.

A gamma ray may be given off by itself, but more usually accompanies alpha or beta radiation.

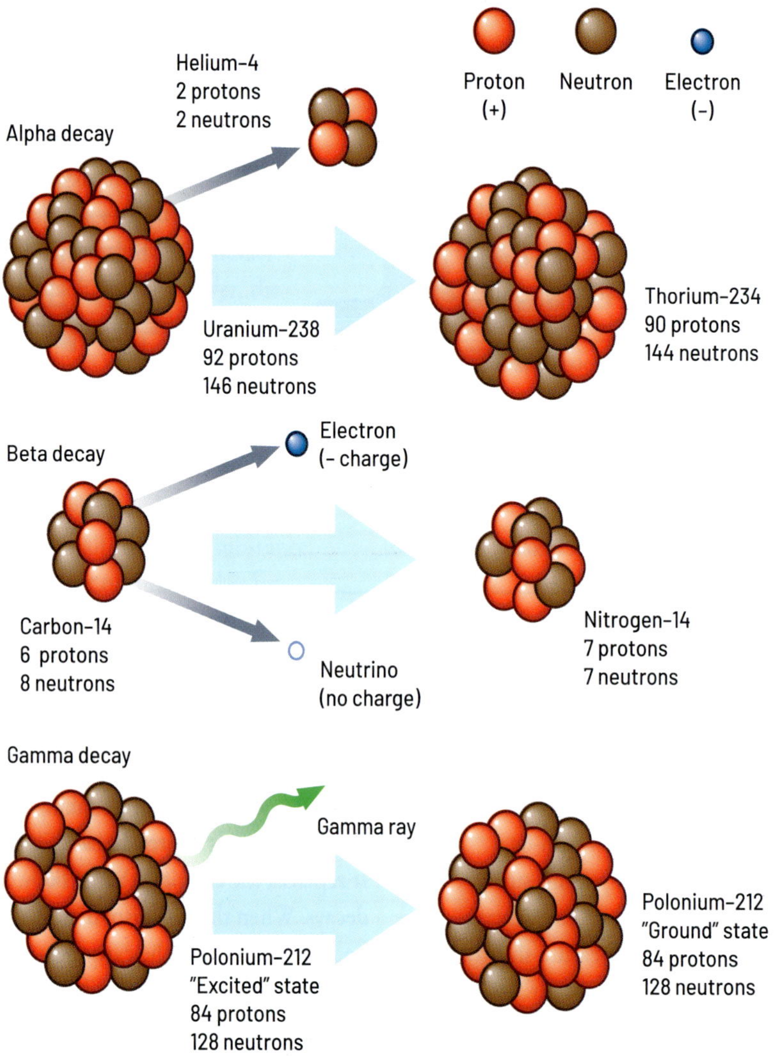

The bones, skin, cloth, and rope of this ancient burial can all be radiocarbon-dated.

CHAPTER 6

Using Isotopes

When scientists learned how to identify and separate isotopes, they were able to use them in a variety of ways. Isotopes are now commonly employed in science and industry. They are also important in modern medicine. They can trace the paths of chemically active substances, revealing the inside of the human body and helping to diagnose diseases.

Some isotopes are strongly radioactive, which makes them useful in various ways. For example, engineers may wish to measure the amount of wear in an engine. The engine is exposed to strong radiation, and itself becomes radioactive. When it is run under

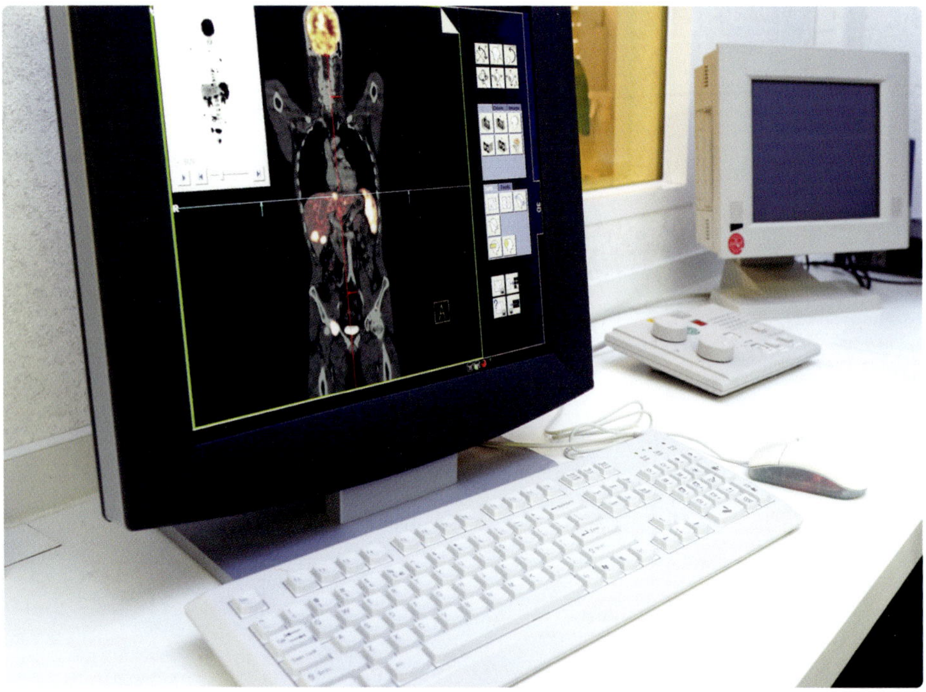

A radioisotope gives a glimpse inside a human body. The radioactive material has been injected into the body and has become concentrated more strongly in some places than in others. The colors indicate the strength of the radiation.

SMOKE DETECTOR

The radioactive material ionizes air molecules, giving them an electric charge so that an electric current can flow between two electrodes. Smoke particles partly block the current, triggering an alarm and a flashing light.

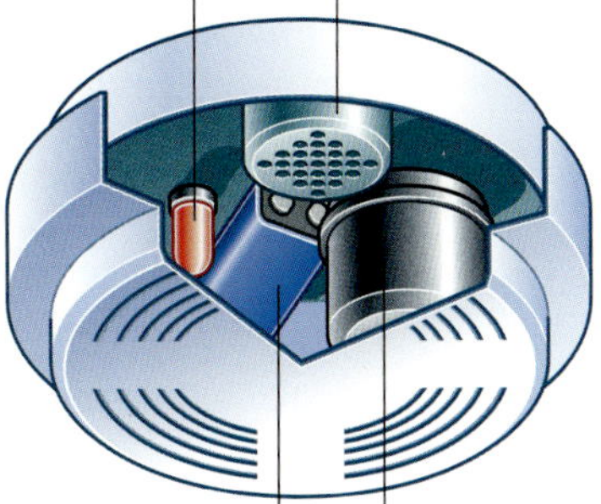

TRACING LEAKS

A leak in an underground gas pipe can be detected with the aid of radioactivity. A slightly radioactive gas is pumped into the pipe. Little radiation can get through the wall of the pipe, but gas escapes into the ground at the leak. Its radioactivity can be detected with a Geiger counter.

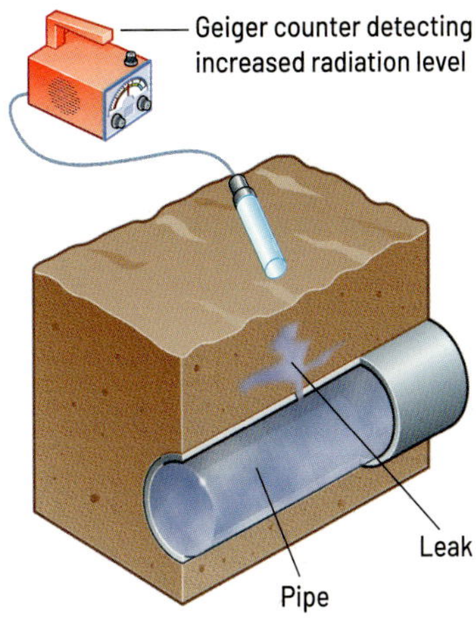

test conditions for a long time, very small quantities of the metal in the cylinders and pistons are worn off and pass into the lubricating oil. The oil can be removed from the engine, and the amount of eroded metal in it can be measured by a radiation detector. That shows how well or badly the engine is wearing.

Radioactive materials can be used to "X-ray" industrial components, such as steel girders or joints in pipes, to produce images that reveal flaws that are invisible to the naked eye.

Biologists study the movement of chemical substances through the bodies of plants and animals. They can use food, for example, that is "labeled" with radioactive carbon-14. Later the radioactivity from carbon-14 atoms will be detected in the body of the organism and in its excretions, giving valuable information about life processes. This type of radioisotope is called a tracer.

Radioisotopes in Medicine

Radioisotopes have many uses in medicine. They can be injected into the body in very small amounts, so that their radiation does not harm the patient. Their movements can easily be traced by detectors that generate a computer image of the body. Places where the isotope concentrates show up on the image.

The radiation from certain isotopes can also be used in the treatment of tumors and other harmful growths. A beam of strong radiation can be narrowly focused, destroying the harmful cells but avoiding damage to the surrounding healthy tissues. Sometimes physicians inject a strongly radioactive material chosen because it will gather at the site of the growth. The material must have a short half-life, so that the radioactivity will not linger in the body and possibly harm the patient.

Studying Ice Cores

Sometimes valuable information can be gained by studying isotopes that are not radioactive. Earth scientists studying the climate of the past have drilled into the ocean floors and obtained long "cores," or cylinders, of rock. The rock is made from the shells of tiny single-celled animals that lived long ago. The scientists measure the ratio of the amount of oxygen-16 (the common isotope) to that of oxygen-18. This ratio is the same as the ratio of the two isotopes in the ocean waters at the time the animal died. It depends on the temperature of the ocean at that time. So measuring the ratio in the rock at a given depth reveals the temperature of the oceans at the time that rock was formed.

Measuring isotopes in ice cores drilled from beneath the north and south polar ice caps also gives information about climate changes in the past.

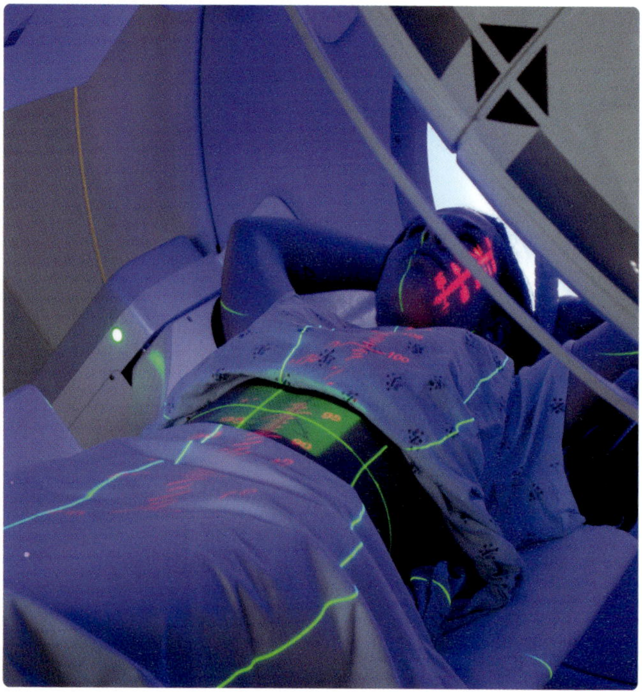

Forms of radiation can be useful in the diagnosis and treatment of illnesses, such as cancer.

This scientist is taking ice core samples from a snow mine under the South Pole.

ALBERT EINSTEIN

The most famous scientist of modern times, Albert Einstein, was born in Germany in 1879. During his lifetime he adopted first Swiss and then U.S. nationality. In 1905, while working in the patents office in Geneva, Switzerland, he published what came to be known as his special theory of relativity, which stated that in a system moving at high speed relative to an observer, time is slowed down and distances are shortened in the direction of motion. He also showed that fast-moving objects gain in mass and that mass is a form of energy. (His famous equation $E=mc^2$ describes how even a tiny amount of mass, m, can be converted into a massive amount of energy, E, which is the basis of nuclear power plants and atomic bombs.) Ten years later, in his general theory of relativity, he linked gravity to time and space, and explained the apparently "wrong" positions of some stars as being due to the bending of space by the mass of the sun.

theory of relativity (see above). As the particles gain mass, they lag behind where they should be and do not arrive at the gap at the moment when the voltage difference is right to boost them. This imposes a serious limit on the amount of energy the cyclotron can give to particles.

This effect is overcome in a linear accelerator, also called a linac (see illustration, page 37). It consists of a series of metal tubes called drift tubes. Rapidly varying voltages are applied to the tubes. Particles are injected at one end. Inside each of the tubes they move at a steady speed, but they are accelerated by a voltage difference as they pass from one tube to the next. The lengths of the tubes are adjusted so that particles reach each gap at exactly the right moment despite their increase in mass.

The largest linear accelerator in the world is at SLAC, the Stanford Linear Accelerator Center at Stanford University, in California. It is 2 miles (3.2 km) long and began working in 1967. The voltage kicks that it delivers to particles are equivalent to a single voltage boost of 50 billion volts.

Particle Racetrack

The problem of particles lagging because their masses increase with speed is also overcome in the synchrotron. Instead of following spiral paths, the particles travel along a "racetrack," a circular hollow tube. Electromagnets guide them along the right path and focus the beam, and electric fields repeatedly give them a boost. Particles go around the machine millions of times, picking up energy with each circuit. The frequency of the applied electric fields and the strength of the guiding magnetic fields have to be increased together as the particles gain energy.

The world's biggest synchrotrons are operated by CERN, which is the major European particle physics laboratory. They are the LEP (Large Electron–Positron Collider) and the LHC (Large Hadron

This scientist is taking ice core samples from a snow mine under the South Pole.

CHAPTER 7

Particle Accelerators

Some of the biggest machines in the world are particle accelerators. They are designed to smash atoms and subatomic particles into each other at high speeds. The collisions create temperatures hotter than the center of a star. A new set of particles is created, which exist for microseconds. The remains of these collisions give scientists information about the structure of nuclei and particles.

Soon after radioactivity was discovered, two French physicists brought it about artificially. Irène Joliot-Curie (daughter of Marie and Pierre Curie) and her husband, Jean-Frédéric Joliot-Curie, bombarded the light element boron with alpha particles and

THE CYCLOTRON

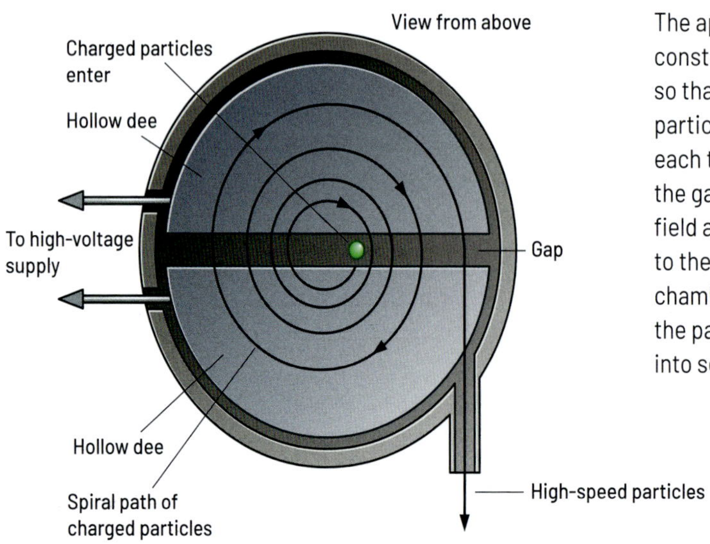

The applied voltages constantly alternate, so that a charged particle gets a boost each time it crosses the gap. A magnetic field at right angles to the plane of the chamber bends the particle's path into semicircles.

THE LINEAR ACCELERATOR

Particles are guided along the accelerator by electromagnets. The voltage of each tube constantly varies in such a way that a particle's speed is boosted as it leaves one and enters the next.

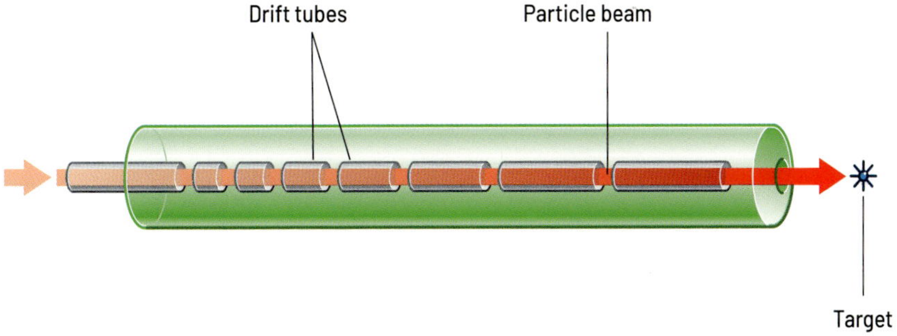

SPLITTING THE ATOM

In 1932 John Cockcroft and Ernest Walton charged a hollow metal chamber to 400,000 volts and injected protons into it. The positively charged particles were driven away from the high positive voltage along a series of tubes kept at lower voltages and struck a piece of lithium. Alpha particles (helium nuclei) formed in the interaction caused flashes on an observation screen.

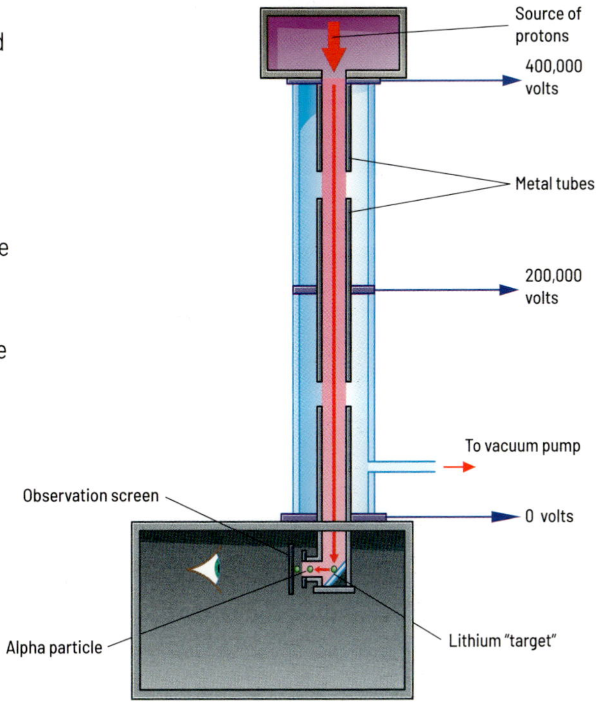

Irène Joliot-Curie was awarded the Nobel Prize in Chemistry in 1935 for her discovery of artificial radioactivity. She shared the award with her husband Jean-Frédéric Joliot-Curie.

found that some of its atoms were turned into those of a radioactive isotope of nitrogen. Together they had succeeded in changing one kind of element into another.

About this time the British physicists John Cockcroft and Ernest Walton built the first particle accelerator (see illustration, page 37). They used it to accelerate protons, letting them hit a target made of the light metal lithium. They found that sometimes protons combined with a lithium nucleus to form a nucleus of an isotope of beryllium, beryllium-8. The new nucleus was unstable and immediately split into two helium nuclei.

Cyclotron

The U.S. physicist Ernest O. Lawrence had already invented a way of accelerating particles that could raise them to even higher energies while using only relatively small voltages. His cyclotron consisted of two

SYNCHROTRON

In the synchrotron, electrons and positrons circulate in opposite directions in the storage ring. They are accelerated until they have enough energy, when the beams are made to collide inside the detector. Some particles are led off and fired at stationary secondary targets.

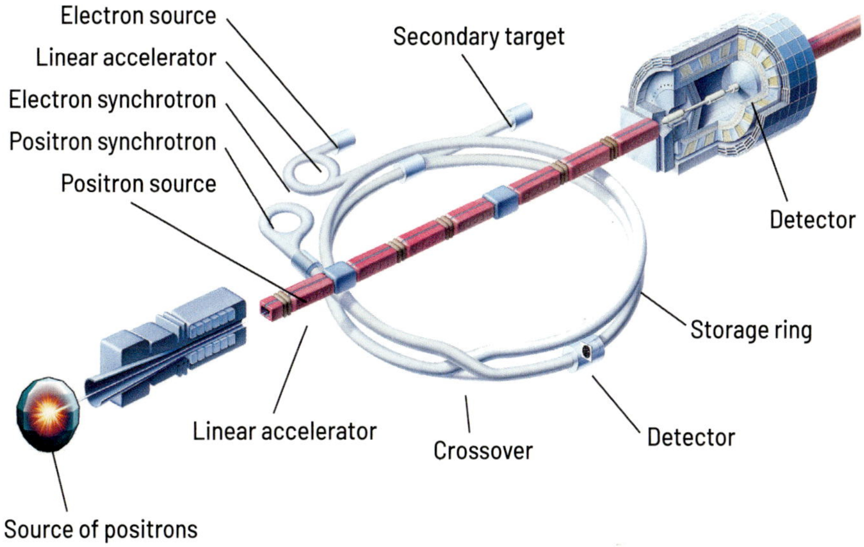

"dees," or D-shaped hollow metal chambers. Charged particles were fed in at the center. A magnetic field at right angles to the dees caused the particles to revolve in a small circle. The dees were kept at different voltages. While inside one of the dees, a particle moved at constant speed because the whole of the dee was at the same voltage. But when it crossed the gap, the particle would get a boost from the voltage difference. While the particle was moving in a semicircular path in that dee, the voltages would be flipped, so that when it again hit the gap it would receive another boost. So the particles spiraled outward, going faster and faster, getting a succession of small kicks from the electric field. By 1939 a cyclotron 5 feet (1.5 m) in diameter had been built that could give particles the energy they would get from a single boost of 19 million volts.

As the particles in a cyclotron go faster and gain more energy, they gain mass. This effect was predicted in Albert Einstein's special

ALBERT EINSTEIN

The most famous scientist of modern times, Albert Einstein, was born in Germany in 1879. During his lifetime he adopted first Swiss and then U.S. nationality. In 1905, while working in the patents office in Geneva, Switzerland, he published what came to be known as his special theory of relativity, which stated that in a system moving at high speed relative to an observer, time is slowed down and distances are shortened in the direction of motion. He also showed that fast-moving objects gain in mass and that mass is a form of energy. (His famous equation $E=mc^2$ describes how even a tiny amount of mass, m, can be converted into a massive amount of energy, E, which is the basis of nuclear power plants and atomic bombs.) Ten years later, in his general theory of relativity, he linked gravity to time and space, and explained the apparently "wrong" positions of some stars as being due to the bending of space by the mass of the sun.

theory of relativity (see above). As the particles gain mass, they lag behind where they should be and do not arrive at the gap at the moment when the voltage difference is right to boost them. This imposes a serious limit on the amount of energy the cyclotron can give to particles.

This effect is overcome in a linear accelerator, also called a linac (see illustration, page 37). It consists of a series of metal tubes called drift tubes. Rapidly varying voltages are applied to the tubes. Particles are injected at one end. Inside each of the tubes they move at a steady speed, but they are accelerated by a voltage difference as they pass from one tube to the next. The lengths of the tubes are adjusted so that particles reach each gap at exactly the right moment despite their increase in mass.

The largest linear accelerator in the world is at SLAC, the Stanford Linear Accelerator Center at Stanford University, in California. It is 2 miles (3.2 km) long and began working in 1967. The voltage kicks that it delivers to particles are equivalent to a single voltage boost of 50 billion volts.

Particle Racetrack

The problem of particles lagging because their masses increase with speed is also overcome in the synchrotron. Instead of following spiral paths, the particles travel along a "racetrack," a circular hollow tube. Electromagnets guide them along the right path and focus the beam, and electric fields repeatedly give them a boost. Particles go around the machine millions of times, picking up energy with each circuit. The frequency of the applied electric fields and the strength of the guiding magnetic fields have to be increased together as the particles gain energy.

The world's biggest synchrotrons are operated by CERN, which is the major European particle physics laboratory. They are the LEP (Large Electron–Positron Collider) and the LHC (Large Hadron

The CERN giant particle accelerator is the largest in the world. Its 17-mile (27 km) underground tunnel straddles the French–Swiss border.

Collider), which share an underground tunnel 17 miles (27 km) in circumference. It straddles the French–Swiss border near the Swiss city of Geneva. The LEP can give electrons and positrons the equivalent of 100 billion volts; the LHC can give protons the energy equivalent of trillions of volts.

Time to Collide

Collisions between subatomic particles can be made far more powerful if two beams of particles can be made to run into each other head-on, rather than firing a beam at a stationary target. Colliders are giant accelerators in which swarms of particles are stored, circulating for hours. For example, a beam of electrons may circulate in one direction, separated from a beam of positrons that circulate in the other direction. When there are enough particles and they have enough energy, the two beams are made to collide head-on.

CHAPTER 8

The Atomic Bomb

In the 1930s, scientists in Europe discovered that uranium atoms could be made to split in two. It was also discovered that a chain reaction in uranium splitting would cause a huge release of cheap energy. However, as World War II loomed, the process became the basis of a fearsome weapon that would cause explosions of unprecedented destructiveness.

Late in 1938 the German physicist Lise Meitner and her nephew Otto Frisch discovered an ominous new form of radioactivity. Other physicists had studied the effects of bombarding uranium, the heaviest known atom, with neutrons to try to make new elements. The results from uranium were puzzling. Meitner and Frisch, both exiled from Germany by the Nazi government, realized that the uranium,

↑ A fireball of hot gas climbs into the sky as an atom bomb is tested. The heat and blast cause immediate devastation, but lingering radioactivity is a threat that lasts for years.

after absorbing a neutron, did not merely emit particles, as most radioactive nuclei did. It became so unstable that it split into two smaller nuclei, such as barium and krypton, while giving out several neutrons.

In 1939, on the eve of the outbreak of World War II in Europe, two Hungarian refugees, Leo Szilard and Eugene Wigner, together with Albert Einstein (see page 40), wrote to the U.S. president, Franklin D. Roosevelt, with a grim warning. They had realized that it might be possible for a chain reaction to occur in uranium in which the neutrons from each fission (splitting) would trigger several

CHAIN REACTION

A slow-moving neutron triggers the fission, or splitting, of a uranium-235 nucleus, and several neutrons are given out. In uranium that has been enriched so that it contains a high proportion of uranium-235, these neutrons soon strike other uranium-235 nuclei and repeat the process. There is a cascade of fissions, with an enormous release of energy.

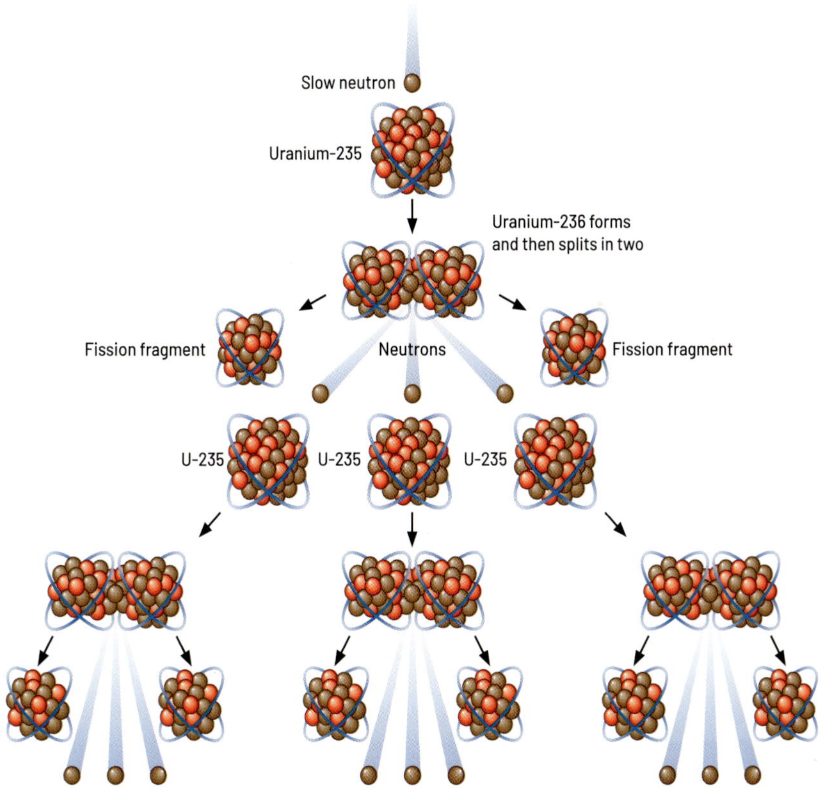

Enola Gay, a B-29 Superfortress bomber, dropped the atomic bomb on Hiroshima on August 6, 1945.

further fissions, and they would cause still further ones, so that there would be an enormous release of energy. Released in a controlled way, this energy could be a boon. Released in a split second, it would cause an explosion of unprecedented destructive power. In 1940, Otto Frisch was working in Britain with another German-born physicist, Rudolf Peierls, on uranium fission. They alerted the British government to the possibility of creating a chain reaction in uranium.

Shortly after entering World War II at the end of 1941, the United States launched an enormous effort to build an atomic bomb before Nazi Germany could. The first test of a bomb using the artificial element plutonium took place in the New Mexico desert in July 1945, two months after the end of the war in Europe. In August, two bombs were dropped on Japanese cities in the Pacific. The first, using uranium-235, fell on Hiroshima and exploded with the force of 13,000 tons (13 kilotons) of conventional high explosive. The second, using plutonium, fell on Nagasaki and had a force of 20 kilotons.

The resulting flood of radiation that poured out from these explosions killed and injured many thousands of people who were exposed to it. It also made vast amounts of radioactive material, which was flung into the sky. This material descended in dust, ash, and rain over the following weeks and months, bringing further death and disease.

The city of Nagasaki was devastated when a second atomic bomb was dropped on Japan on August 9, 1945.

CHAPTER 9

Nuclear Reactors

The first step on the road to building an atomic bomb was to show how a chain reaction of uranium could be started and then managed. The man who did this was Italian-born physicist Enrico Fermi. He built the world's first nuclear reactor in a squash court at the University of Chicago. Since then, nuclear reactors have become a major source of energy for many of the world's nations. There are various types that are now in operation. However, many people are opposed to nuclear reactors because of the dangers they can pose.

This first reactor was a giant assemblage of blocks of graphite, a form of carbon, some of the blocks containing cylinders or spheres of uranium. The reactor was called a "pile." Neutrons were continually being produced by the radioactive uranium. They would pass through the graphite and be slowed down (or "moderated") to boost the chance of a chain reaction. The slowed neutrons traveled onward, entered another piece of uranium, and triggered fission in the rare isotope uranium-235.

← The first atomic pile, built at the University of Chicago, was literally a pile of blocks of natural uranium and graphite.

ENRICO FERMI

The leader of the team that achieved the first chain reaction was a brilliant Italian-American, Enrico Fermi.

Born in Rome in 1901, Fermi won the Nobel Prize in Physics in 1938 for his work on the production of artificial radioactivity by bombarding elements with neutrons. He had in fact split the uranium atom, although he did not clearly understand that at the time. Fermi went straight from the Nobel prize-giving ceremony in Stockholm, Sweden, to the United States. He feared the policies of Italy's Fascist government.

When the huge American effort to build an atomic bomb was launched during World War II, Fermi led a team of scientists and engineers at the University of Chicago. After achieving the world's first artificial chain reaction, he worked at Los Alamos on the building of the atomic bombs.

After World War II, Fermi opposed the development of the hydrogen bomb on moral and technical grounds. He died in 1954 at the age of 53. Element number 100 on the is named fermium after him.

In December 1942 the first chain reaction was achieved. It was not enough to generate useful power, but it showed what was possible. A coded message was sent to colleagues in the bomb-making project, reading, "The Italian navigator has entered the New World." It meant that chain reactions were possible, and the drive began to build atomic bombs.

New Energy Source

After World War II ended in 1945, scientists and engineers began working to make nuclear fission a source of cheap and plentiful energy (although others continued to build still more fearsome nuclear weapons). All fission reactors worked on the same basic principles, although they used different sorts of fuel, different ways of controlling the reaction, and different ways of converting the reactor's heat into electricity.

Some types of reactor use enriched uranium, in which the proportion of uranium-235 has been raised from its normal value of 0.7 percent to, typically, 3 percent. Most of the fuel consists of the common isotope of uranium, uranium-238. The fuel is contained in long, thin rods with corrosion-resistant casings. The rods can be withdrawn and replaced when fresh fuel is needed.

The neutrons given out by the uranium-238 have to be slowed down so that they can trigger fission in the uranium-235 nuclei. The neutrons given out by the uranium-235 also have to be slowed to continue the chain reaction. That is done by means of a substance called a moderator. Moderators include graphite—as in the first pile— and heavy water, which is water in which part of the hydrogen consists of the rare isotope deuterium.

The heat generated in the reactor core is used in any of various different ways to boil water, so that the steam can drive a turbine, which generates electricity.

CANDU REACTOR

The CANDU heavy-water reactor was developed in Canada to use natural uranium. Heavy water is pumped through the reactor core. It moderates the neutrons—that is, it slows them down and makes the chain reaction possible. The water is heated by the high temperature in the reactor, and the heat is used to generate steam to drive turbines.

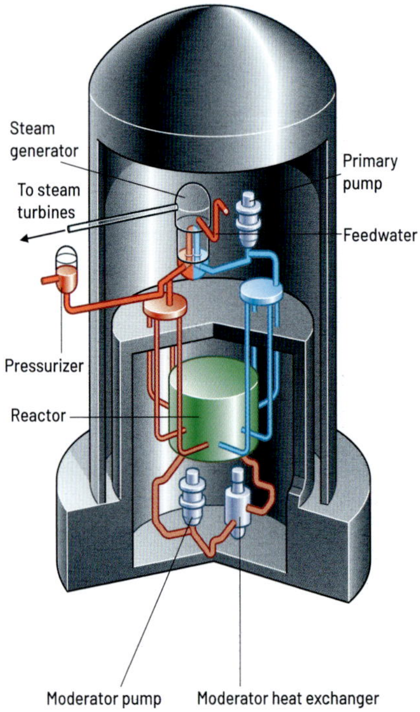

AGR REACTOR

The AGR (Advanced Gas-Cooled Reactor) is a British design. The fuel is enriched uranium, the moderator is graphite, and the coolant is carbon dioxide gas.

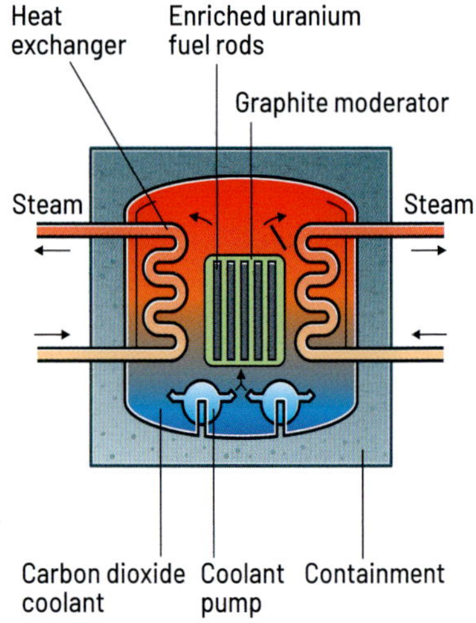

Different Reactors

Most of the world's reactors are PWRs, or pressurized-water reactors. In this type of reactor the coolant is ordinary water that is kept under high pressure so that it does not boil. It is also the moderator, slowing neutrons to promote the reaction. The water circulates in a closed loop. On leaving the reactor core this water is highly radioactive. It is at an extremely high temperature and gives up its heat to water in a separate system. It is this water that boils and drives turbines. The fuel is enriched uranium.

The CANDU (CANadian Deuterium–Uranium) heavy-water reactor was developed in Canada to compensate for the fact that Canada did not then have access to enriched uranium. The neutrons from the natural uranium, which is mostly uranium-238, need to be slowed down to make them cause fission. Heavy water is the coolant and moderator. Plutonium is produced by the fission of uranium, and itself fissions to provide about half of the total energy output.

The Advanced Gas-cooled Reactor (AGR) was developed in Britain. It uses enriched uranium as a fuel, graphite as the moderator, and carbon dioxide gas as the coolant. The design is intended to be safer than reactors using water as a coolant. In an accident water could boil, and then the core would overheat. Carbon dioxide coolant cannot change its state and would therefore do its job under all circumstances.

PWR REACTOR

In the American-designed PWR (Pressurized-Water Reactor) the coolant is superheated water. It is kept under 150 atmospheres of pressure, typically, to prevent it from boiling. The water circulates in a closed circuit, giving up its heat to boil water circulating in a separate system. The reactor and the heat exchanger are kept inside a strong containment building in case of an explosion.

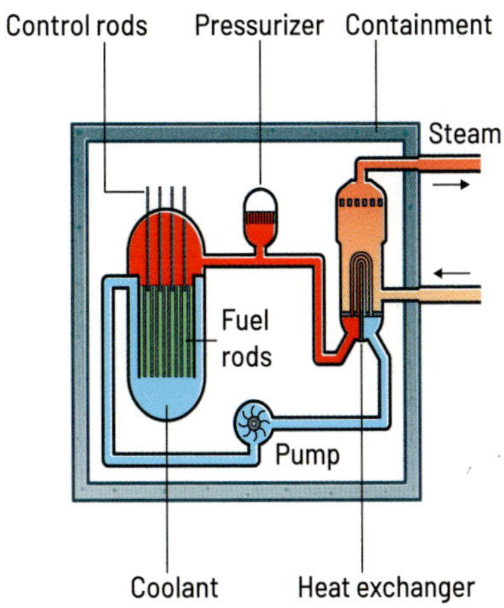

FAST BREEDER REACTOR

A fast breeder reactor converts uranium-238 into plutonium. The coolant is molten sodium or other liquid metal, which is good at transferring heat, but does not slow down neutrons.

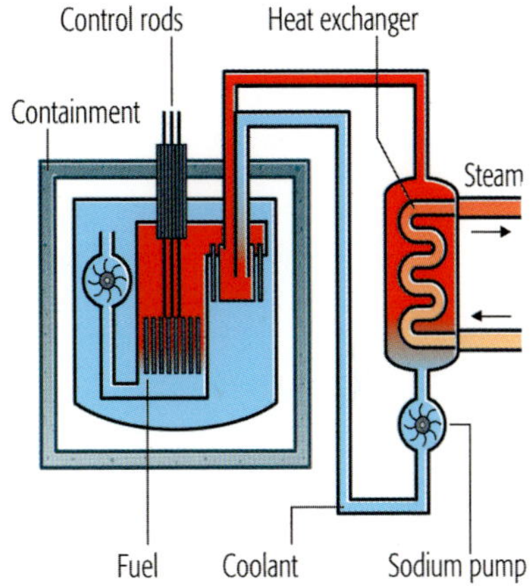

Energy and Fuel

Ordinary nuclear reactors use only about 1 percent of the energy that theoretically could be obtained from uranium. It is possible to extract more energy in a "breeder" reactor, which both supplies energy and converts uranium into fuel. Typically, a uranium nucleus absorbs a neutron and then gives out two electrons (beta particles) in succession. Losing these

WIDESPREAD CONTAMINATION

After the Chernobyl explosion radioactive gases and ash from the blazing reactor core were spread across Western Europe by winds (see map on the opposite page). As far west as Britain, sheep were declared unfit to eat as a result of contaminated rainfall. How many deaths resulted from this airborne radioactivity is not known.

The contamination was so great because the reactor lacked a containment building, so its lethal radioactive core was exposed to the atmosphere. The reactor used graphite as a moderator and ordinary water as a coolant. The heat from the core caused the water to boil, and the steam was used to drive turbines directly.

This photo shows the wrecked reactor building at Chernobyl after the explosion of April 1986.

SPREAD OF CHERNOBYL RADIOACTIVITY

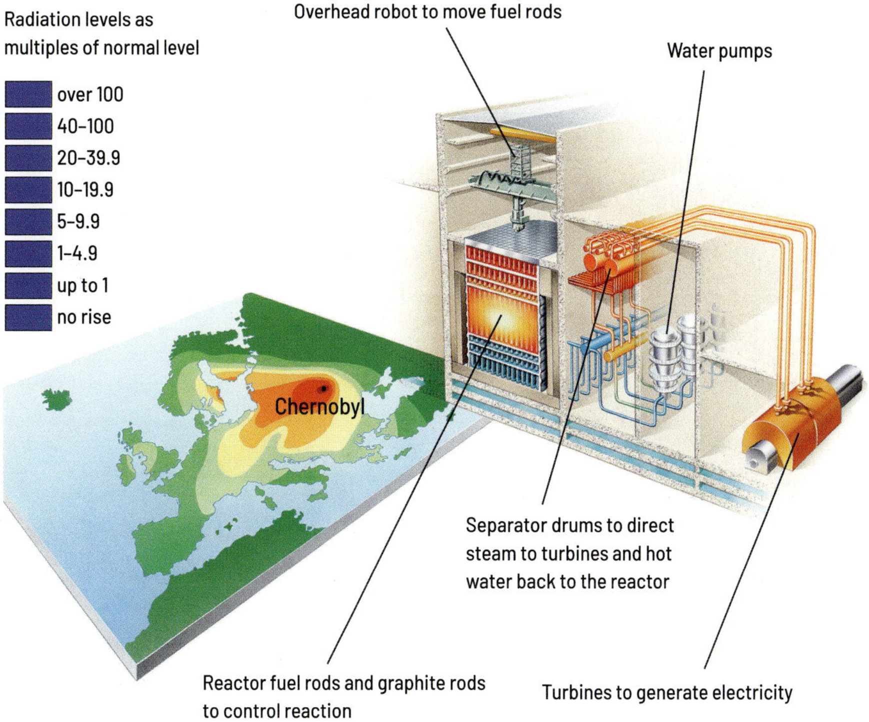

two negative charges means that its own charge increases by 2, so that it becomes a nucleus of element 94, plutonium. This can be used as a fuel.

In one type of breeder reactor fuel rods containing a mixture of uranium and plutonium produce heat. Liquid sodium metal is used as the coolant, and there is no moderator. Neutrons leaving the fuel enter a surrounding layer of uranium, which is partially converted into plutonium. The reactor produces slightly more fuel than it consumes.

Understanding the Dangers

Opposition to nuclear power grew steadily from the 1960s as the public became aware of the dangers that could arise with this technology. A nuclear reactor cannot explode in the same devastating way as an atomic bomb. Any explosion would scatter the fuel before more than a tiny fraction had fissioned—the intricate design that goes into a warhead is needed to prevent this from happening. But if the cooling systems in a reactor fail, the reactor core will overheat, leading to possible "meltdown." There can

The buildings near Chernobyl, such as this school, remain abandoned.

be an explosion that will scatter highly radioactive material over the surrounding area and perhaps high into the air, where the wind can carry it for great distances.

Three Mile Island

Such an incident occurred in the PWR at Three Mile Island in Pennsylvania in 1979. Some of the pressurized-water coolant was lost, and the reactor's automatic cooling systems switched on. However, because of human error this system was shut off, and the core overheated and was badly damaged. Radioactive gases escaped from the reactor and the local authorities came close to ordering mass evacuation. For some hours there was near-panic in the surrounding area. The resulting public outcry led to severe regulation and placed such stringent difficulties in the way of building reactors in the United States that no new ones have been built there since 1978. Some that were under construction at the time were abandoned.

The city of Pripyat was abandoned a few days after the Chernobyl disaster.

Chernobyl Disaster

In April 1986, disaster struck one of the four reactors operating at Chernobyl in Ukraine, part of what was then the Soviet Union. The reactor exploded, blowing off the roof, and its core began burning fiercely. Radioactive material was poured into the sky and over the surrounding area. Inadequately protected personnel heroically fought the blaze. In a few days most of these people had fallen ill and died. Helicopters dropped liquid concrete onto the gaping wound of the reactor core, finally entombing it. Soviet authorities said that 31 people died within a short period of the accident, but an unknown number developed fatal disease in the following months and years. Winds blew the nuclear pollution westward, and neighboring countries in Europe experienced many days of fear.

CHAPTER 10

Uses for Nuclear Energy

Nuclear power is an efficient way of creating electricity. It can heat water to produce steam that drives turbines in electricity-generating plants. Smaller nuclear reactors have also been constructed to drive machines. Some ships and submarines contain small nuclear reactors to drive the turbines that power the propellers. The challenge is to control radioactivity.

There are various designs of nuclear reactor, which differ mainly in the coolant they use. One of the greatest problems facing the designer of a practical nuclear power plant is the radioactivity of the reactor. Neutrons from the fission processes penetrate thick layers of most materials. To shield the outside world from these neutrons there is always a protective shield, called a biological shield, surrounding

The huge concrete dome of the reactor containment building dominates this nuclear power plant. A dome is the best shape for resisting pressure and containing radioactive gas if there is an explosion.

ELECTRICITY GENERATION

Just as in coal- or oil-fired power stations, nuclear power stations use the heat they generate to produce steam. This drives turbines, which drive electrical generators.

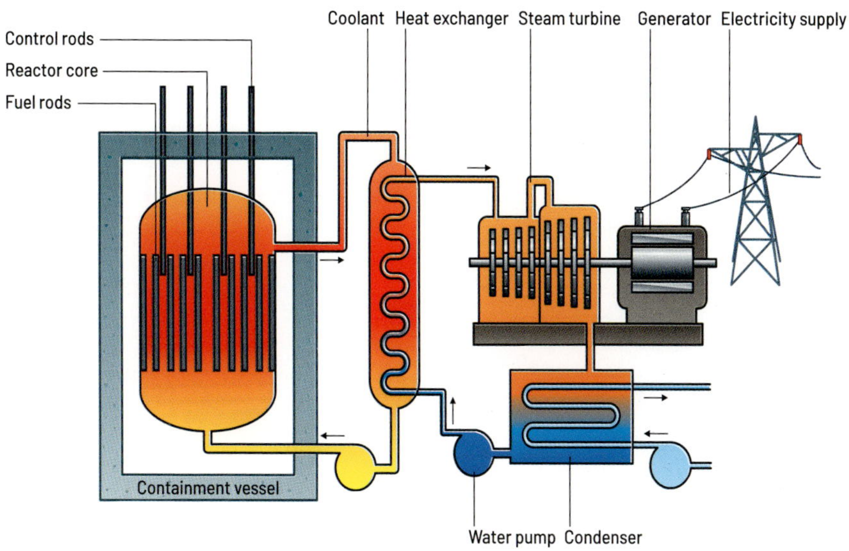

the reactor. But the coolant—fluid that flows through the reactor and takes away its heat to be used—becomes intensely radioactive.

In boiling-water reactors (BWRs) ordinary water is used as the coolant. It boils in the reactor, and the steam drives turbines directly. In other types of reactor the coolant flows in a closed circuit and so makes no direct contact with the outside world. It is led around other pipes carrying water, which is heated to boiling point. The steam from the boiling water drives turbines. Each turbine consists of a series of wheels carrying blades. As the hot steam flows through the turbine it forces the wheels to spin, driving an electricity generator. After passing through the turbines, the steam is still hot and at quite a high pressure. It then needs to be condensed—turned back into water—to go around the circuit and be boiled again. It is cooled by being passed over other pipes carrying cold water from some external source such as a nearby river or lake.

Controlling Reactions

The reactor fuel is contained inside long, thin metal rods, which can be lowered into the reactor core. Between them are other rods of some neutron-absorbing substance, such as cadmium. As more control rods are

This Russian nuclear-powered icebreaker was designed to keep Arctic sea lanes open and clear of ice.

lowered into the reactor core, more neutrons are absorbed and the reaction is damped down. As the control rods are withdrawn, the reaction goes faster. In an emergency many control rods can be inserted into the reactor rapidly in order to shut it down immediately.

In case of an accident or explosion, the nuclear reactor is enclosed in a massive concrete and steel containment building with a large dome. The structure is designed so that it will withstand even a powerful explosion inside the reactor building.

Nuclear Pros and Cons

Some dangers of nuclear power have been mentioned previously. If the core were to overheat, there would be a chance of an explosion that would spread radioactive materials into the environment. There is also the major problem of disposing of the radioactive wastes that remain when fuel has been used up. (This is more fully discussed in the next chapter.) However, nuclear power has advantages over other forms of energy generation. In normal operation there is almost no contamination

PRESSURIZED-WATER REACTOR SYSTEM

The pressurized superheated water that circulates through the reactor is kept separate from the water that is boiled to make steam. When the steam leaves the turbine it is condensed as it passes around pipes through which water is pumped from a river or lake.

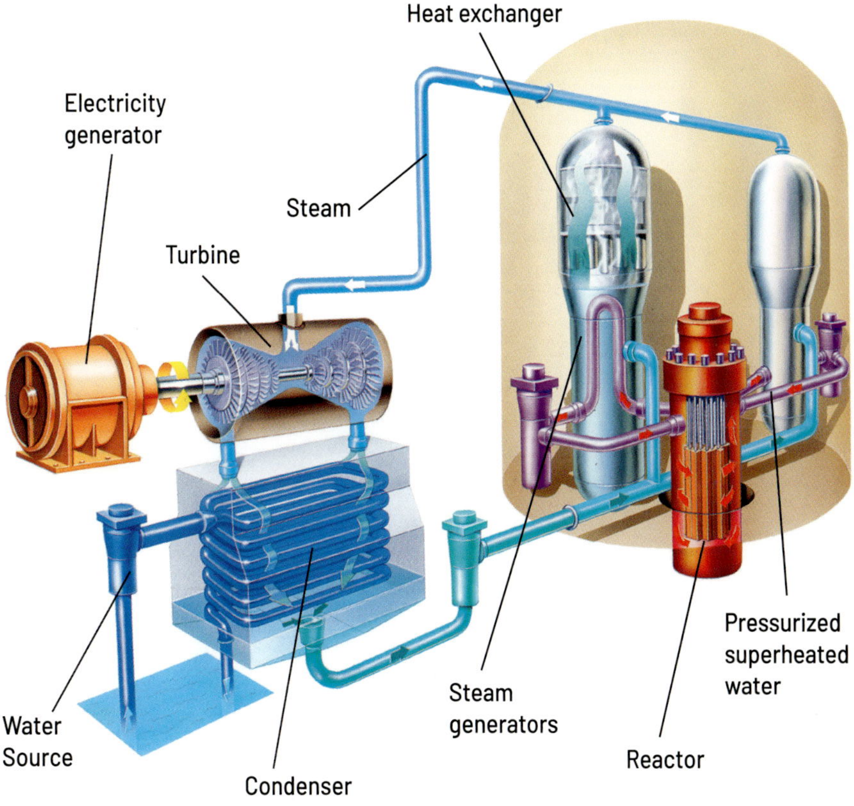

of the environment. Coal- and oil-powered generation stations pour out smoke, causing atmospheric pollution that results in millions of deaths worldwide every year. Cleaning the output gases from conventional power stations is an expensive luxury that only the richest countries can afford.

One major benefit of nuclear energy is that it does not produce greenhouse gases. These are gases, notably carbon dioxide, that trap the heat of sunshine in the atmosphere. Although there are many natural sources of greenhouse gases, some are also given out by industrial processes, including conventional

Air pollution and smog are major problems in many cities, such as Beijing.

energy generation, by highway traffic, and by agriculture. The world's climate has warmed in the last few decades, and most scientists agree that this is probably due to the greenhouse gases that the industrialized countries are pouring into the atmosphere. Nuclear power plants don't produce such gases during operation, although mining and processing their fuel and removing their waste does produce a small amount of greenhouse gas.

Although there are centuries of coal reserves, oil, and gas will run out relatively soon. However, there is enough uranium ore to last for centuries if used in breeder reactors. And renewable sources of energy, such as sunlight, wind, and waves, cannot produce the quantities of energy that nuclear energy can. Having as many different forms of energy supply as possible makes a country less vulnerable if one source of energy is cut off by an unfriendly government.

Fear of the dangers of nuclear energy has brought the building of new nuclear power plants to a halt in the United States and some other countries, but nuclear energy programs are vigorously pursued elsewhere. There are more than 400 nuclear power plants throughout the world. A major nuclear country is France, which uses nuclear power plants to provide about two-thirds of its energy. Many developing countries are building up their nuclear industries, although this is often partly to provide them with material for nuclear weapons.

Other Uses

Nuclear fission has other uses than supplying cities with electricity. It is used in some large ships, including several U.S. aircraft carriers and Russian icebreakers. These ships need not be refueled for years at a time. Submarines carrying strategic missiles have long been nuclear powered, so that they can not only stay at sea for years at a time, but can also do so while submerged. The nuclear reactors do not need air, unlike conventional diesel engines.

Nuclear reactors produce huge quantities of neutrons, which in power plants are stopped by the biological shield. Some research laboratories have reactors so that

Many countries are very dependent on nuclear power. France has 56 nuclear power plants, including the nuclear power plant seen here.

On March 11, 2011, an earthquake occurred off the coast of Japan. It caused a tsunami. The tsunami flooded and damaged the Fukushima Daiichi nuclear power plant, releasing dangerous nuclear energy into the air.

scientists can carry out research using neutrons. Neutrons can be used for making a great range of radioisotopes. They have uses in medicine, both for treatment and for imaging, and in industry (see chapter six).

In the early days of nuclear energy journalists often predicted that "atomic planes" and "atomic cars" were just around the corner. We will never see them, because a reactor and its shielding have to be very heavy. There are compact power units, called radioisotope thermoelectric generators, that use energy from radioisotopes. Radioactive decay generates a steady supply of heat. This is converted into electricity. But there is no chain reaction, so the principle is different from that of the nuclear reactor. Only a small amount of power can be supplied by such generators, but they are valuable for use in artificial satellites and space probes.

CHAPTER 11

Making Waste Safe

Nuclear reactors produce waste material. This waste is highly dangerous and remains radioactive for centuries. As more use is made of the benefits of nuclear energy, safely disposing of the waste products is vital for the health of the planet and future generations.

The problem of waste disposal looms over the nuclear energy industry. At every stage of the nuclear fuel cycle, from mining the ore to disposing of spent fuel, deadly radioactive wastes are produced that must somehow be made safe.

Uranium is obtained from a variety of ores, including pitchblende, carnotite, and coffinite. The ore has to be milled, or ground up, and the parts that are richer in uranium are sent on for processing. What remains is only slightly radioactive, but must be securely buried. The result of the enrichment process is that enriched ore (containing a few percent of uranium-235) is passed on to the fuel-fabrication process. The rest of the ore, containing about 0.3 percent uranium-235, is called depleted uranium and

Radioactive waste management involves a series of stages: waste treatment; packaging in special containers or drums for safe storage; storage facilities for at least 50 years; and final permanent storage underground.

is either disposed of or used as part of the fuel in breeder reactors. The enriched uranium, possibly together with partly spent fuel from working reactors, is made into pellets that are loaded into corrosion-proof fuel rods, ready to be taken to the power plant.

Waste Treatment

"Burned" fuel removed from a reactor contains unused uranium-235. It is kept underwater in storage tanks for a while before some of it is sent to long-term storage; the remainder goes for reprocessing. The enriched portion of the reprocessed fuel is added to other fuel for reuse in reactors. The depleted portion is sent to long-term storage.

The waste from nuclear reactors consists of intensely radioactive isotopes formed during the fission process. This radioactivity cannot be reduced by chemical or physical processing. After being combined with other substances to make a chemically unreactive glass-like material, the waste is buried somewhere it will not be damaged. Some of this material will be dangerous for thousands of years.

These containers of spent fuel are being transported by rail in the UK.

NUCLEAR FUEL REPROCESSING CYCLE

Uranium ore consists mostly of uranium-238. It is mined, milled (ground up), and concentrated before being shipped. The ore is then enriched to increase the percentage of uranium-235 present. In the fuel fabrication process the enriched uranium, together with reprocessed fuel, is made into pellets and loaded into fuel rods. In the reactor, some uranium-235 is used up, while plutonium is created. Spent fuel is reprocessed to retrieve some "low-enriched" uranium and plutonium. The highly radioactive "high-level waste" will have to be stored deep underground for centuries.

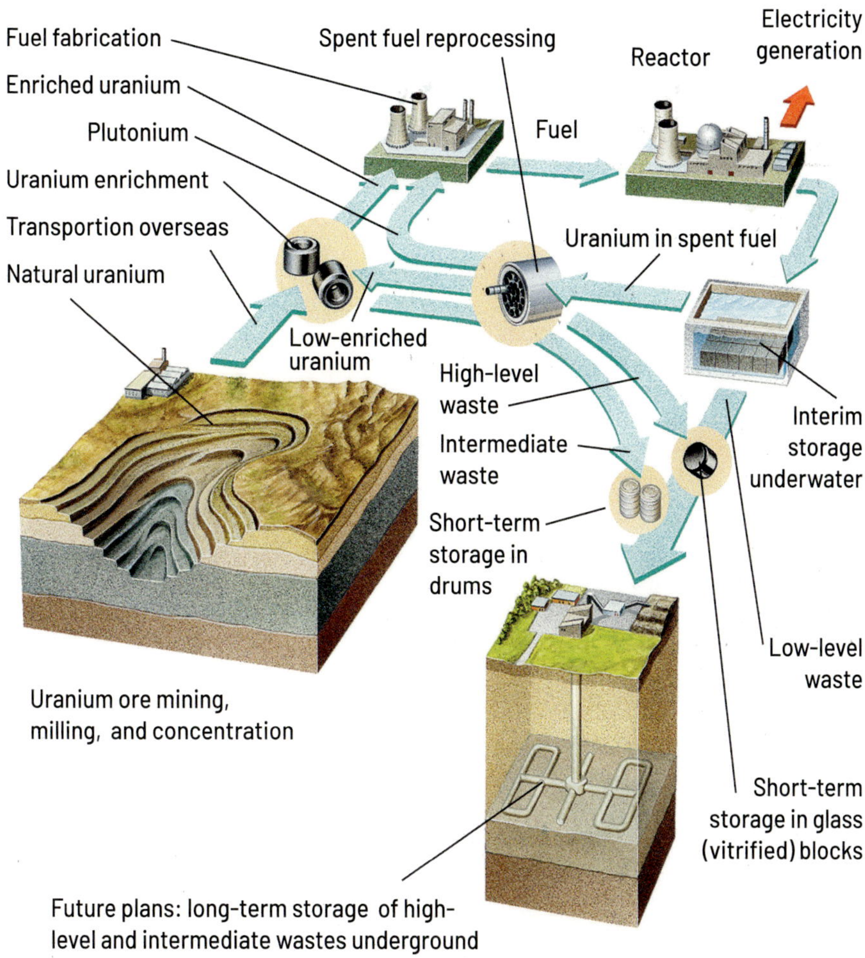

CHAPTER 12

The Sun, Hydrogen, and Helium

In nuclear fission, a heavy nucleus such as uranium is split into lighter nuclei (with a few other particles also produced). The atoms and particles have less mass than the original uranium atom. The difference in mass is turned directly into energy, as first described by Albert Einstein.

But there is another way of releasing nuclear energy. Low-mass nuclei can be combined to make a more massive one. If the new nucleus has less mass than the sum of the masses of the original nuclei, then again the surplus mass must be turned into energy. That is what happens in the Sun and other stars.

Sun

The center of the Sun is at a pressure about 250 billion times the pressure of our atmosphere at ground level and a temperature of about 25 million °F (15 million °C). Whole atoms cannot exist in these conditions, and they are

← There are more than 100 billion stars in our galaxy, the Milky Way. The stars are natural fusion reactors in which light nuclei are welded into heavier ones.

torn apart into nuclei and electrons. So the center of the Sun is a swarm of charged particles, which scientists call a plasma. The plasma consists mostly of single protons and electrons. There are also helium nuclei, each consisting of two protons joined to two neutrons. Protons smash into each other and build up heavier nuclei in a series of reactions, ending with helium nuclei. During these reactions energy is given out.

Hydrogen

Other stars are much like the Sun. Low-mass stars burn more slowly than the Sun and so are fainter. High-mass stars burn much faster and more brightly. In these massive stars other reactions occur, but with the same end result: hydrogen nuclei are turned into helium nuclei.

Helium

At the end of a star's life the hydrogen fuel runs low, and it begins to burn helium to form heavier nuclei, which are in turn burned, forming even heavier elements (see page 8).

FUSION IN THE SUN AND ON EARTH

In the Sun (below left) hydrogen is fused to form helium via the proton-proton reaction. First, two protons collide. One proton emits a positron (a positively charged electron) and turns into a neutron. The proton and neutron join together, forming deuterium, an isotope of hydrogen. Later, another proton collides with the deuterium nucleus, forming another isotope of hydrogen, tritium, consisting of a proton joined to two neutrons. Later, two tritium nuclei collide and finally form a helium-4 nucleus (two protons joined to two neutrons) and two free neutrons. In addition, photons and neutrinos are given out throughout the chain of processes. In a tokamak-type fusion reactor (see page 67) a different reaction is used (below right). Deuterium and tritium nuclei injected into the reactor collide to form a helium-4 nucleus and a neutron. Both processes release vast amounts of energy as heat and light.

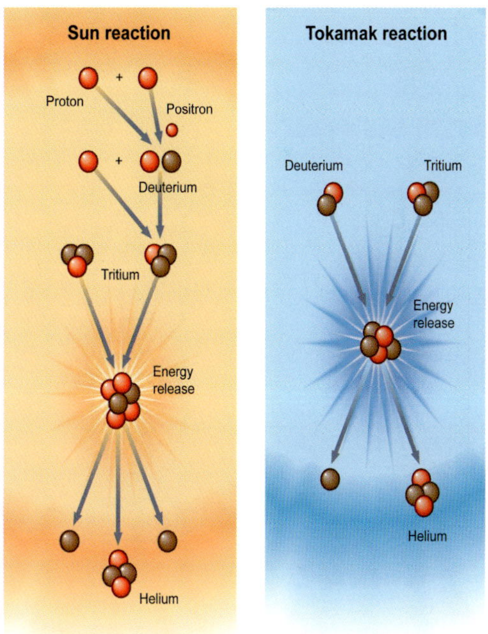

CHAPTER 13

Nuclear Fusion

If scientists can find a way of making nuclear fusion possible on an industrial scale, then the world's energy problems will be solved. There would be no need to use fossil fuels or nuclear fission. The isotopes of hydrogen that are found in water could be harnessed to provide plentiful sources of energy. However, so far, the technical problems involved in creating nuclear-fusion reactors have proven commercially unviable.

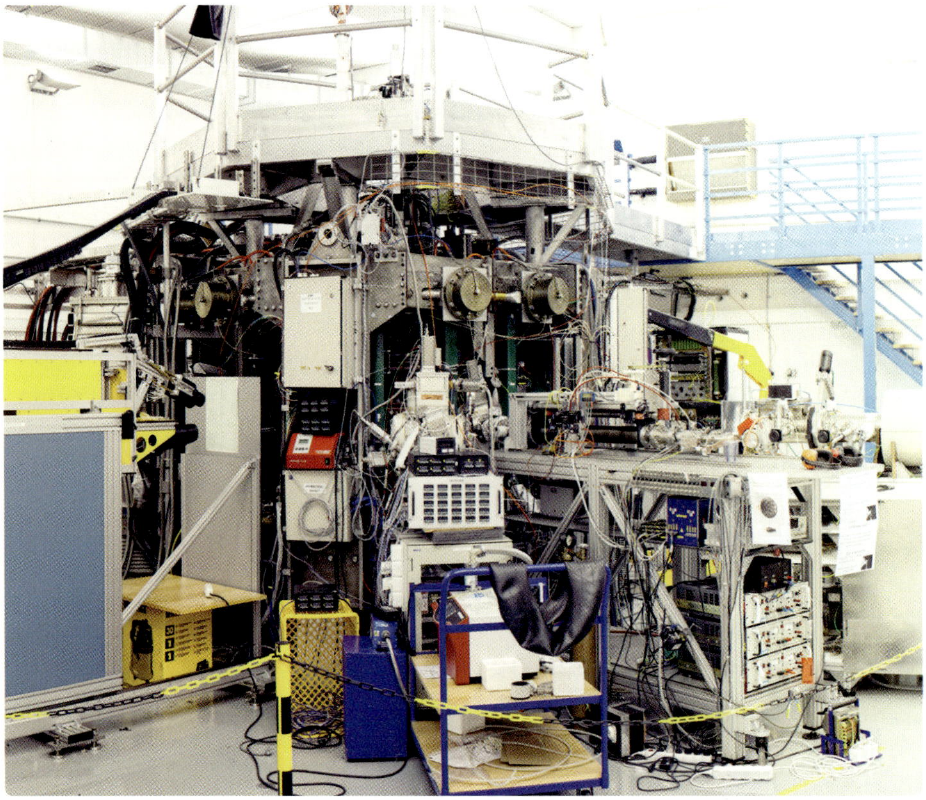

↑ In this fusion reactor, called a tokamak, powerful magnetic fields keep a plasma bottled up while raising it to high temperatures.

HOW A TOKAMAK WORKS

Like a household transformer, the tokamak's transformer converts alternating currents (AC) in one circuit (the primary coil) into AC in another, secondary, "coil," which is actually the plasma current. The field coils also help to create and guide the plasma current.

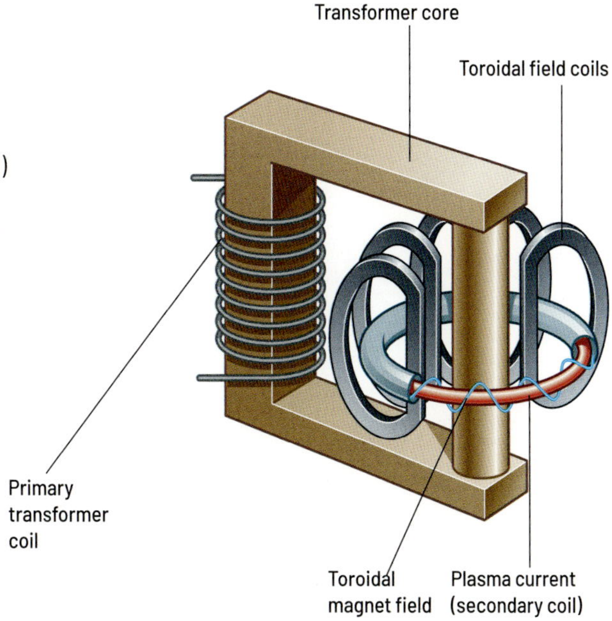

Nuclei must be forced together at high speeds to overcome the electric repulsion between them. In the center of the sun the plasma is under tremendous pressure and at high temperature. In a fusion reactor on Earth it is possible to create even higher temperatures—hundreds of millions of degrees, as compared with the Sun's 15 million °C. But instead of the huge pressure, magnetic fields must be used to hold in the plasma and prevent it from touching the walls of the reactor, which would melt at the very high temperatures.

No practical fusion reactor has yet been built. Experimental designs have managed to achieve the necessary reactions, but don't

A MAGNETIC BOTTLE

Hot plasma must not touch the walls of a fusion reactor or it would instantly lose heat. Suitably shaped magnetic fields can trap the charged particles.

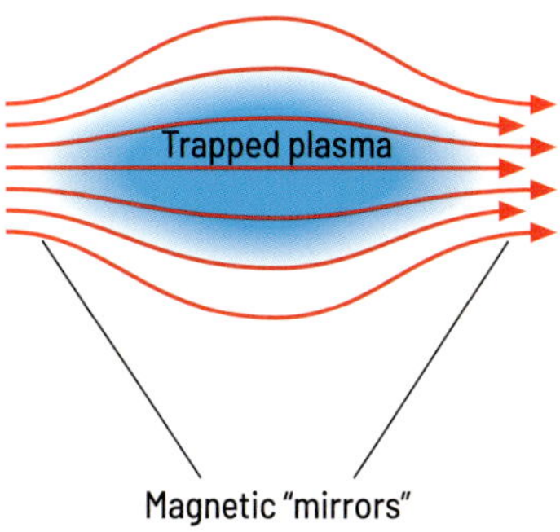

A technician works in a dust-free environment on an experimental laser-fusion installation.

yet produce enough energy to make them commercially viable.

Magnetic Confinement

The most heavily researched fusion reactor design, the tokamak, was developed in Russia. It uses powerful alternating currents to create pulsed magnetic fields that heat up a plasma and keep it circulating inside a torus (a hollow ring, something like a doughnut). In one design for a working reactor of the future, the gases deuterium and tritium are continuously fed into a tokamak torus, and the helium produced is drawn off. The fusion reactions send out floods of neutrons that penetrate the walls of the plasma's torus and are absorbed by a blanket made from the metal lithium. The neutrons react with the lithium, generating heat that is used to turn water into steam to drive turbogenerators.

Inertial Confinement

In a completely different design of fusion reactor, pellets containing deuterium and tritium are blasted with intense laser beams from many directions. For a fraction of a second extreme pressures and temperatures are reached, and the elements fuse to form helium and release energy. This was the approach used in the LL National Ignition Facility (NIF) in California, which produced a breakthrough in fusion in 2022. The NIF project finally achieved an energy milestone when it produced an energy profit (more energy output than the energy fed into it).

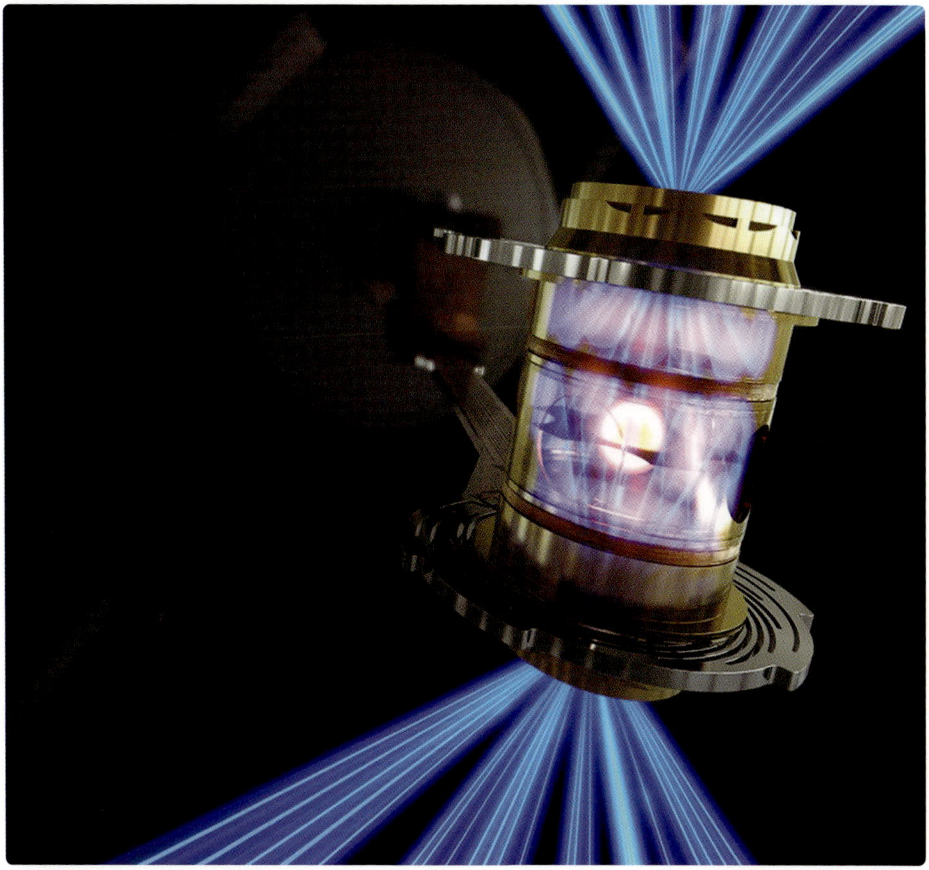

In inertial fusion, the deuterium-tritium mix is contained in a pellet the size of a peppercorn positioned inside a cylinder. Powerful lasers focus on the walls of the cylinder to create the conditions in which a fusion reaction can occur inside the pellet.

A nuclear bomb exploding in the ocean.

CHAPTER 14

BIOGRAPHY

Julius Robert Oppenheimer

In 1943, the American nuclear physicist Julius Robert Oppenheimer became director of the Manhattan Project. This was a U.S. government research program set up to develop atomic weapons. Oppenheimer and his team created the first atomic bomb, and he is sometimes referred to as the "father" of the atom bomb. His later opposition to the creation of the even more destructive hydrogen bomb, alongside his political views, led to his being investigated by a U.S. military security committee in 1953.

Julius Robert Oppenheimer was born into a wealthy New York family. He attended Harvard University and, like most promising young American physicists of the day, went on to complete his scientific education in Europe. He attended the universities of Cambridge in England, Göttingen in Germany, Leiden in the Netherlands, and Zurich in Switzerland. While at Cambridge he wanted to study under Ernest Rutherford (1871–1937), the pioneer of subatomic physics, but he was rejected. Oppenheimer obtained his

← Julius Robert Oppenheimer was a brilliant scientist and was influential in the development of the atomic bomb.

KEY DATES

1904 April 22, born in New York
1925 Graduates from Harvard University, Cambridge, Massachusetts
1927 Receives doctorate from Göttingen University, Germany
1938 Nuclear fission is first observed
1942 The Manhattan Project to develop an atomic bomb is set up by the U.S. government
1943 Oppenheimer becomes director of the Manhattan Project laboratories based at Los Alamos, New Mexico
1945 July 16, first atom bomb successfully tested
1952 First hydrogen bomb tested
1953 Oppenheimer's security clearance is withdrawn
1955 Publishes *The Open Mind* summarizing his philosophical ideas on science and society
1963 Awarded the Atomic Energy Commission's highest honor, the Fermi Prize
1967 Dies in Princeton, New Jersey

Ph.D. at Göttingen at the time Werner Heisenberg (1901–1976) was developing his theory of quantum mechanics there. Back in the United States in 1928, Oppenheimer became assistant professor of physics at the University of California at Berkeley, where he developed theoretical physics (the study of matter and energy based on reasoning from known data rather than experimentation). He also held a position at the California Institute of Technology, in Pasadena.

Early Career

Among Oppenheimer's early work was the study of neutron stars. It was already known that stars with a mass greater than that of the sun would eventually collapse to such a degree that their electrons and protons—the negatively and positively charged elementary particles within them—would be crushed together to make neutrons, or neutral elementary particles. This would produce a "neutron star." Oppenheimer argued that such stars would collapse even further to become what would later be described as "black holes," stars so dense that not even light can escape them. In the 1930s this theory was regarded as being too far-fetched to be taken seriously. It was not until the later 1960s that black holes became a major subject of research.

Splitting Atoms

In 1938 the German chemist Otto Hahn (1879–1968) was working with the element uranium. Uranium is the heaviest of the natural elements; its atoms are unstable—short-lived or radioactive. In 1934, Italian physicist Enrico Fermi (1901–1954) had found that when uranium is bombarded by subatomic particles called neutrons, several radioactive products are formed; he thought that they were radioactive isotopes similar to uranium 235. Hahn took Fermi's work a stage further. He found that one of the products of bombarded uranium was a radioactive form of the much lighter element barium. Hahn sent an account of his work to his colleague Austrian physicist Lise Meitner (1878–1928), who proposed that the production of barium

THE FIRST CHAIN REACTION

The first controlled, self-sustaining chain reaction took place on the squash court at Stagg Field, University of Chicago, Illinois, under the direction of the Italian- born U.S. physicist Enrico Fermi (1901-1954). A chain reaction is produced when an atomic nucleus is bombarded by neutrons to cause nuclear fission.

In order to create the fission reaction, Fermi and his team built a simple nuclear reactor. Rods of natural uranium were placed in a large pile of 40,000 graphite blocks; the huge structure soon became known as "the pile." The purpose of the graphite was to slow down the fast neutrons emitted during fission so that they were more likely to cause further fissions than to escape from the pile. A number of rods made of cadmium were included to absorb stray neutrons and to prevent a premature chain reaction from taking place.

On December 2, 1942, the cadmium control rods were slowly removed. Counters set up to measure the rate of neutron production began to click; soon the clicks were so rapid that they became a continuous buzz, and Fermi confirmed that a chain reaction had started. Before there was any danger of a massive explosion, the cadmium control rods were replaced and the reaction halted. The success of Fermi's dramatic experiment was relayed to other nuclear scientists in a coded message from his team announcing "The Italian navigator has just landed in the New World."

was the result of the nucleus of the uranium atom being split in two to form two lighter nuclei. At the same time it emitted two or three neutrons, and released a large amount of energy. This was evident because the mass of the elements produced—barium and krypton—was slightly less than that of the original uranium. The "missing" mass had been converted into energy.

Elements that are capable of undergoing fission are known as fissionable. In further experiments, Hahn and Meitner found that the rarer U-235 isotope is more fissionable than the U-238 isotope that makes up 99.3 percent of natural uranium. Isotopes are atoms that have the same number of protons but a different number of neutrons in their nuclei. Once the reaction is set off in U-235, one neutron causes the release of three more neutrons. Any of these new neutrons can now collide with another U-235 atom, so releasing another three neutrons, each of which can release three more neutrons, and so on, until there is no uranium left. This is called a chain reaction. The process is very rapid; within less than a millionth of a second there is a massive release of energy.

Fearing the Bomb

World War II (1939–1945) was about to break out in Europe, and some scientists in Britain and the United States were quick to see that the nuclear fission process might be used to create an extremely powerful bomb.

office bugged by FBI agents throughout the period that he was working with the Manhattan Project. In August 1943, in a bizarre episode that has never been properly explained, Oppenheimer told military security agents that he had heard how secret information could be passed to Russia. He claimed that Soviet agents had approached two of his colleagues, and he implicated a friend, a professor at Berkeley, who was subsequently dismissed from his post. At security clearance hearings nearly a decade later Oppenheimer declared that what he had said in 1943 was "a tissue of lies."

Meanwhile work was continuing on the Manhattan Project, with scientists facing a number of immense problems, both theoretical and practical. The first was how to produce enough fissionable U-235. Because U-235 and U-238 are chemically identical, they had to be separated physically.

A separation plant was set up near Knoxville, Tennessee; this was later known as the Oak Ridge Plant. It was engineering on a heroic scale: the plant made use of electromagnets 246 feet (75 meters) long. The separation processes to produce just a small amount of fissionable U-235 required complicated machinery and vast amounts of electric power. An alternative fissionable isotope—plutonium 239—had been created at the University of Chicago by American

The Los Alamos National Laboratory is still a center of nuclear research in the United States.

physicist Arthur Holly Compton (1892–1962) and Enrico Fermi, the nuclear physicist who had been responsible for the first controlled chain reaction at Stagg Field (see page 73). This involved redesigning the reactor pile to produce plutonium 239—a highly complex process that required the building of massive chemical reactors. Huge production reactors were later constructed for this purpose at the Hanford Plant, an isolated 1,000 square-mile (2,590 sq m) area of land on the Columbia River north of Pasco, Washington.

Dangers and Deaths

A chain reaction will cause an explosion only if there is a certain minimum amount of fissionable material; this is called the "critical mass." The problem was to assemble a critical mass without it exploding on its own. The real dangers of this work were tragically illustrated by two early fatalities at Los Alamos. In the first, a young laboratory worker Harry K. Daghlian (1921–1945) accidentally handled radioactive material during a critical mass experiment; he died of radiation sickness 26 days later. On May 23, 1946 Canadian physicist Louis Slotin (1913–1946) was carrying out a risky procedure known in the laboratory as "tickling the dragon's tail." This involved causing two huge metal hemispheres of highly reactive beryllium-coated plutonium to approach each other while readings were taken. On this occasion Slotin's screwdriver slipped and the two masses came too close together. Slotin tore them apart with his bare hands as the laboratory filled with a blinding flash of blue light. He died nine days later.

Tests and First Use

The first atomic bomb was tested on July 16, 1945 at a site in the New Mexico desert called Trinity. The bomb, given the name "Fat Man" because of its shape, was located at the top of a steel tower and scheduled to go off at 5:30 in the morning. Many of the project scientists watched the explosion from just 5 miles (8 km) away—no one then knew of the risks of exposure to radiation fallout.

Eyewitnesses described the momentous event. The physicist Otto Frisch noted: "And then without a sound the Sun was shining; or so it looked." Oppenheimer recalled: "There floated through my mind a line from the Bhagavad-Gita [an epic Indian poem], "I am become death, the shatterer of worlds." The explosion lit up the sky, and 40 seconds later a shock wave resounded down the valley. Fermi scattered scraps of paper as the explosion hit, calculating from the distance they were blown that the bomb must have generated a power equivalent to about 20,000 tons of TNT explosive. The steel tower was almost completely destroyed.

Less than a month later, on August 6, 1945, an atomic bomb using U-235 was dropped on the industrial port of Hiroshima, on the main Japanese island of Honshu, killing an estimated 80,000 civilians. Three days later a second atomic bomb using plutonium was dropped on Nagasaki. About 40,000 people were killed instantly. On August 15, Japan surrendered unconditionally, bringing World War II to an end. Within a year another 150,000 victims had died as a result of the explosions and, for decades after, thousands more died of radiation sickness.

Babies would be born with defects as the result of genetic mutations caused by exposure to radioactive fallout. At the time of the drop, however, people knew very little about the long term consequences of radiation. Nevertheless, Oppenheimer resigned from his position at the Manhattan Project in October 1945.

Superbomb

Edward Teller, who worked on the Manhattan Project from 1942 to 1946, had long argued in favor of developing a hydrogen bomb (H-bomb), which would be still more powerful than the atomic bomb, by combining deuterium and tritium, isotopes of hydrogen (the lightest element) to create a helium nucleus (helium is the second lightest element). This process is called nuclear fusion. On August 29, 1949 the Soviet Union announced it had exploded its first fission bomb. Teller repeated his call for a "superbomb", as he termed it.

Oppenheimer was by now chairman of the General Advisory Committee of the Atomic Energy Commission. In October 1949 it officially stated its opposition to the development of the hydrogen bomb, concluding that there was "no limit to its explosive power" and that it would go much

↑ During World War II the Fuller Lodge at Los Alamos was used for social gatherings. Today it houses the Los Alamos Historical Museum.

This building in Hiroshima is one of the few buildings that was left standing near the center of the atomic blast. Today it is part of the Hiroshima Peace Memorial.

further than the atomic bomb in terms of exterminating civilian populations. However, President Harry S. Truman (1884–1972) was persuaded by Teller and others that there was no alternative but to develop the H-bomb. The need to beat the Soviet Union in this new arms race had become of paramount importance.

On November 1, 1952 the first hydrogen bomb was exploded by the United States at Eniwetok Atoll, Marshall Islands, in the Pacific Ocean. The bomb created a 5,250-foot (1,600-m) wide crater. Its explosive power was 500 times greater than the bomb that had been dropped on Nagasaki. On August 12, 1953 the Soviet Union claimed to have exploded a hydrogen bomb. Although its design was in fact fairly unsophisticated, the shock of finding that the Soviet Union was pulling ahead in the weapons race heightened the storm of fear against communism already raised by the McCarthy hearings.

Charged and Cleared

Questions were asked about why the Atomic Energy Commission and Oppenheimer, its chief scientist, had been so slow to support

The film *Oppenheimer* was a box-office success in 2023. It dramatized the complex relationship between Robert Oppenheimer and the U.S. political and scientific establishment.

the development of the H-bomb. On December 21, 1953 a list of charges were leveled against Oppenheimer: that he had mixed with communists; that he had recruited communists to Los Alamos; that he had tried to delay work on the H-bomb; and that he was probably a Soviet spy. His security clearance, which allowed him access to secret information, was removed.

Oppenheimer, determined to clear his name, chose to go before a security hearing. He was found not guilty of treason, but his security clearance was not returned and his post as adviser to the Atomic Energy Commission was terminated. One of those who testified against him was Teller.

Although Teller had insisted that Oppenheimer was "loyal to the United States," he added that he would "prefer to see the vital interests of this country in hands that I understand better and therefore trust more." His action enraged other scientists, and the Federation of American Scientists protested against Oppenheimer's trial.

Oppenheimer's reputation was restored in 1963 when, as a gesture of apology for the treatment he had received, he was awarded the Atomic Energy Commission's highest honor, the Fermi Prize, which he collected from President Lyndon B. Johnson (1908–1973) at the White House. Oppenheimer died four years later of cancer of the throat.

SCIENTIFIC BACKGROUND

Before 1930

The French physicists Henri Becquerel (1852–1908), Marie Curie (1867–1935), and Pierre Curie (1859–1906) pioneer the study of atomic radiation

The New Zealand-born British physicist Earnest Rutherford (1871–1937) and the Danish physicist Neils Bohr (1885–1962) develop models of the atom in which a nucleus of protons (positively charged particles) is orbited by electrons (negatively charged particles)

The German-born physicist Albert Einstein (1879–1955) predicts that matter can be converted into energy

1932 English physicist James Chadwick (1891–1974) discovers a neutral atomic particle, the neutron

1932 The positron (antielectron), a particle that is exactly like an electron but behaves as if it has a positive charge, is discovered; the existence of such antiparticles was predicted in 1928 by English physicist Paul Dirac (1902–1984)

1934 Italian physicist Enrico Fermi (1901–1954) discovers that when uranium is bombarded with neutrons, several radioactive products are formed

1938 German physicist Otto Hahn (1879–1968) finds that a radioactive form of the much lighter element barium is produced when the uranium atom is bombarded

1939 Otto Hahn's student Lise Meitner (1878–1968) confirms that Hahn has "split" the uranium atom, and calculates that large amounts of energy can be produced by this process, called nuclear fission

1940 In Birmingham, England, two German refugee physicists, Otto Frisch (1904–1979) and Rudolf Peierls (1907–1995), establish that only a few pounds of uranium-235 would be necessary to make an atomic chain reaction possible

1942 At the University of Chicago, the first controlled, self-sustaining nuclear chain reaction is achieved by Enrico Fermi

1943 The main laboratories of the Manhattan Project, the Allied project to develop an atomic bomb, are set up at Los Alamos, New Mexico; Oppenheimer is scientific director

POLITICAL AND CULTURAL BACKGROUND

1925 The first exhibition of Surrealist art is held in Paris; it includes work by the Spanish artists Pablo Picasso (1881–1973) and Joan Miró (1893–1983)

1932 At the Olympic Games in Los Angeles 18-year-old American typist Mildred "Babe" Didrikson (1914–1956) wins gold medals in the javelin and the 80-meter hurdles and a silver medal in the high jump

1933 In Germany a crackdown on any area of the arts that does not conform to Nazi theory leads to the burning of books that are "un-German" or by Jewish authors, and the closure of the influential Bauhaus school of design

1936 Civil war breaks out in Spain as General Francisco Franco (1892–1975) sets up a rival government. He will rule the entire country from 1939

1938 The House Un-American Activities Committee, set up by the House of Representatives to investigate political extremism, focuses almost exclusively on the perceived "communist infiltration" of American society

1941 Japanese bombers attack the American Pacific fleet at anchor in Pearl Harbor, Hawaii, prompting the United States to enter World War II (1939–45)

1943 In the largest tank battle in history, at Kursk, south of Moscow, the Soviet Red Army inflicts a massive defeat on the Germans

1944 Japanese pilots begin launching kamikaze ("divine wind") suicide missions on Allied ships; in 1,465 Japanese attacks more than 3,000 Allied sailors are killed

Glossary

accelerator A machine that accelerates elementary particles to speeds high enough that they can react with one another when they collide.

AGR Abbreviation for advanced gas-cooled reactor, a nuclear reactor in which heat is removed from the hot core by carbon dioxide gas.

antiparticle A particle that has properties opposite to those of the corresponding ordinary particle. For example, an antiproton is like a proton, but negatively charged, while a positron is like an electron, but positively charged.

atom The smallest part of a chemical element that can exist on its own. It has a central nucleus, surrounded by electrons.

atom bomb A bomb that uses the energy of nuclear fission. The nuclei of atoms of uranium or plutonium split, producing enormous quantities of energy.

atomic number The number of protons in an element's nucleus. It equals the number of electrons in the normal atom and is also the element's numerical position in the periodic table.

atomic weight *see relative atomic mass.*

background radiation Weak radiation that is always present around us. It consists mostly of cosmic rays and radioactivity from rocks, with a small proportion of radioactivity in the air from past atomic bomb tests and byproducts of the nuclear industry.

breeder reactor A type of nuclear reactor that not only releases energy but also converts ordinary uranium, which cannot be used in reactors, into plutonium fuel. The plutonium can then be used in other types of reactor to produce still more energy.

bubble chamber A device that makes the tracks of elementary particles visible. It contains liquid hydrogen, kept just below its boiling point. When a charged particle passes through it, bubbles of hydrogen form along its path.

CANDU Abbreviation for Canadian deuterium-uranium nuclear reactor, a reactor that uses heavy water as both the coolant and moderator, and natural uranium as the fuel.

centrifuge A machine with a fast-spinning chamber that creates strong "artificial gravity" to separate materials of different densities. It is used in the enrichment of uranium to make nuclear fuel.

chain reaction A series of nuclear reactions in heavy atoms, such as those of uranium and plutonium, in which a nucleus splits, emitting several neutrons that collide with other nuclei causing them to split and emit further neutrons.

cloud chamber A device that makes the tracks of elementary particles visible. It contains air saturated with water vapor. When an electrically charged particle passes through it, drops of liquid water form along its path.

collider An accelerator designed to fire streams of elementary particles at one another head-on, to increase the energy of their collision.

control rod A rod of a material that can be lowered into a nuclear reactor to absorb neutrons and slow down the chain reaction.

coolant A liquid or gas that is passed around the hot fuel in a nuclear reactor to absorb its heat The coolant is then used to boil water to make steam, which drives turbines to generate electricity.

cosmic rays Subatomic particles and photons that constantly bombard Earth. They originate in high-energy processes in the Sun and other stars.

decay The spontaneous change of one kind of atom into another one while giving out energy. The most common form of the rare metal radium gives out alpha rays and turns into the gas radon.

electron A negatively charged elementary particle found in every atom.

elementary particle A subatomic particle, one of the various particles that make up atoms. The "elementary" implies a particle that is not composed of any other particles, but in fact it is applied more widely—for example, protons and neutrons are called elementary particles, even though they are now known to be made of quarks.

energy The ability of a system to bring about changes in other systems. Atomic nuclei give out energy in the form of fast-moving particles or electromagnetic radiation, such as X-rays. When the particles or rays are absorbed in matter, their energy is turned into heat.

enrichment The partial separation of different isotopes of a nuclear fuel, so that the part that contains more of the useful isotope can be used in a reactor or in a nuclear weapon.

fission The splitting of a heavy atomic nucleus into two roughly equal parts, releasing energy.

force A pushing or pulling action that changes the shape, position, or movement of an object.

fuel rod A rod made of a nuclear fuel such as enriched uranium or plutonium. Fuel rods are removed when the fuel has been used up.

fusion The merging of two light nuclei to form a heavier one, with the release of energy.

gamma rays The shortest-wavelength, highest-energy type of electromagnetic radiation, given out in some kinds of radioactivity.

gas diffusion A technology used in the enrichment of materials used in nuclear reactors and nuclear weapons.

Geiger counter A radioactivity detector. When a fast-moving charged particle such as an electron passes through it, an audible click is produced.

half-life The time it takes for half the nuclei in a sample of radioactive material to decay. Half-lives range from millions of years for some isotopes to fractions of a second for others.

heavy water Water that contains heavy hydrogen, a rare isotope of hydrogen whose atoms are approximately twice as heavy as those of ordinary hydrogen.

hydrogen bomb A bomb that uses the energy of nuclear fusion. The nuclei of atoms of hydrogen are welded together, producing enormous quantities of energy.

light water Ordinary water, containing the common isotope of hydrogen.

mass number The total number of protons and neutrons in the nucleus of a particular isotope.

meson An elementary particle that consists of two quarks.

moderator A material that moderates, or reduces, the speed of neutrons produced in the fission of fuel nuclei in a nuclear reactor. The slower-moving neutrons bring about further fissions, thus making a chain reaction.

molecule A group of atoms linked together, the smallest part of a chemical element or compound that can exist by itself.

neutrino An elementary particle that is produced, along with electrons, in beta decay. It is uncharged, has a very small mass, and hardly reacts at all with other particles. Enormous numbers of neutrinos from space pass through Earth (and your body) every second.

neutron An elementary particle that is electrically neutral (uncharged) and has approximately the same mass as the proton. Outside the nucleus it decays into a proton, an electron, and an antineutrino (the antiparticle of a neutrino).

nucleus (plural nuclei) The positively charged central part of an atom, made up of protons and (except in the common isotope of hydrogen) neutrons, and containing most of the atom's mass.

periodic table An arrangement of the chemical elements according to their chemical properties. An element's position in the periodic table is its atomic number, which is equal to the number of protons in its nucleus.

photon A "particle" of electromagnetic radiation. A photon has a definite amount of energy, which is proportional to its frequency and inversely proportional to its wavelength.

plasma A fluid consisting of ions. Electromagnetic forces make a plasma behave differently from a gas. Nuclear fusion takes place in plasmas in the Sun and stars, and in tokamaks and other fusion machines.

positron The antiparticle of the electron, having the same mass but positive charge.

proton An elementary particle that is positively

charged and has approximately the same mass as the neutron. Protons are found in the nuclei of all atoms.

PWR Abbreviation for pressurized-water reactor, the most common type of nuclear reactor, in which the coolant is ordinary water, kept under high pressure so that it does not boil. The water is also the moderator, slowing neutrons to promote the reaction.

quark A type of elementary particle, of which protons, neutrons, and mesons, among others, are made. Quarks are so strongly bound to each other that they probably never occur singly.

radioactive dating A method of finding the age of rocks or archeological remains by measuring how much of the radioactive material in them has undergone decay since they were formed. *see also half-life; radioactivity.*

radioactivity The emission of particles or radiation by atomic nuclei, which (except with gamma rays) change into other kinds of nuclei as a result.

radiocarbon An isotope of carbon in which there are two extra neutrons in the atomic nucleus. The carbon decays with a half-life of 5,730 years. It is important in dating archeological finds.

radioisotope An isotope of an element that is radioactive.

reactor A device for generating energy, either by nuclear fission or by nuclear fusion.

relative atomic mass The mass of an atom expressed in atomic mass units (amu). The atomic mass unit is defined as one-twelfth of the mass of the common isotope of carbon and is approximately equal to the mass of the hydrogen atom.

storage ring A particle accelerator in which the particles circulate for many hours, building up in numbers, until they can be collided with another particle stream.

synchrotron The most powerful type of accelerator, in which the particles follow a fixed circular path, their speed being boosted by electric fields while their paths are guided by magnetic fields. The LHC is an example.

tokamak A fusion reactor in which nuclei of isotopes of hydrogen, kept confined by magnetic fields, collide at a high temperature and form nuclei of helium, releasing energy.

wavelength The distance between two successive locations where a wave is at its maximum intensity.

Further Information

International Atomic Energy Agency
Vienna International Centre
P.O. Pox 100
A-1400 Vienna, Austria
+43 (1) 2600-0
Website: http://www.iaea.org/
This group, part of the United Nations, is the world's center of cooperation in the field of nuclear physics. It was organized in 1957 under the idea of "atoms for peace," based in part on a speech by US President Dwight D. Eisenhower, with the goal of promoting safe, secure, and peaceful nuclear developments.

Los Alamos National Laboratory
P.O. Box 1663
Los Alamos, NM 87545
505-667-5061
Website: http://www.lanl.gov/index.php
The Los Alamos National Laboratory was established in 1943 to design and build the atomic bomb. Today the laboratory is home to a variety of research programs with the aim of maintaining the country's nuclear capabilities and a focus on national security.

Nagasaki Atomic Bomb Museum
7-8 Hiranomachi
Nagasaki City, Japan 852-8117
+81 (0) 95-844-1231
Website: https://nabmuseum.jp/
On August 9, 1945, the United States dropped an atomic bomb on the city of Nagasaki, Japan. World War II was brought to an end, but the city of Nagasaki suffered greatly. Exhibits include daily life in Nagasaki before the bomb, the devastation caused by the blast, and an area that encourages visitors to consider a world without nuclear weapons.

Atomic Museum
755 E. Flamingo Rd.
Las Vegas, NV 89119
702-409-7366
Website: https://www.atomicmuseum.vegas/
This museum, part of the Smithsonian Institute, traces the conception, development, and testing of the atomic bomb. Exhibits on such topics as radiation and underground testing are on permanent display.

Nuclear Energy Agency (NEA)
46, quai Alphonse Le Gallo
92100 Boulogne-Billancourt
France
+33 1 45 24 78 50
Website: http://www.oecd-nea.org/
This is a specialized agency within a group called the Organisation for Economic Cooperation and Development, or OECD. The OECD is made up of 31 countries across Europe, North America, and the Asia-Pacific region, including France, Sweden, Mexico, Turkey, and the United States.

World Nuclear Association
York House
23 Kingsway,
London WC2B 6UJ, United Kingdom
+44 (0) 20 7451 1520
Website: http://www.world-nuclear.org/
This organization, based in the United Kingdom, represents people and organizations involved in nuclear power around the world. Their Web site includes basic information on nuclear power as well as charts, outlines, and scientific papers with up-to-date information about nuclear power.

Pearl Harbor National Memorial
National Park Service
Peal Harbor National Memorial
1 Arizona Memorial Place
Honolulu, HI 96818
808-422-3399
Website: https://www.nps.gov/perl/index.htm
This national park commemorates the losses suffered in the Japanese attack on Pearl Harbor on December 7, 1941. Visitors can tour exhibit galleries exploring what led up to the attack on Oahu as well as its aftermath, as well as walk through a Remembrance Circle. Visitors can also take a shuttle boat to the USS *Arizona* Memorial, which floats atop the wreckage of the USS *Arizona*, where 1,177 sailors and marines lost their lives.

Publisher's note to educators and parents: Our editors have carefully reviewed these websites to ensure that they are suitable for students. Many websites change frequently, however, and we cannot guarantee that a site's future contents will continue to meet our high standards of quality and educational value. Be advised that students should be closely supervised whenever they access the internet.

Further Reading

Berger, Gary S. and Di Ruggiero, Michael. *Einstein: The Man and His Mind*. Damiani, 2022.

Gray, Theodore. *The Kid's Book of the Elements. An Awesome Introduction to Every Known Atom in the Universe.* Black Dog and Leventhal, 2020.

Groueff, Stephane. *Manhattan Project: The Untold Story of the Making of the Atomic Bomb.* Plunkett Lane Press, 2023.

Hourly History. Robert Oppenheimer: A Life from Beginning to End. Hourly History, 2022.

Katz, Susan B. *The Story of Albert Einstein: An Inspiring Biography for Young Readers.* Callisto Kids, 2020.

Kelly, Cynthia C. *The Manhattan Project: The Birth of the Atomic Bomb in the Words of its Creators,* Eyewitnesses and Historians. Black Dog and Leventhal, 2020.

Miles David. *Atom: The Building Block of the Universe.* Bushel and Peck Books, 2021.

Moss, Marissa. *The Woman Who Split the Atom: The Life of Lisa Meitner.* Harry N. Abrams, 2022.

Murray, Raymond and Holbert, Keith E. *Nuclear Energy: An Introduction to the Concepts, Systems and Applications of Nuclear Processes.* Butterworth-Heinemann, 2019.

O'Daly, Anne. *The Basics of Atoms and Molecules.* Core Concepts. Rosen Publishing, 2024.

Plokhy, Serhil. *Atoms and Ashes: A Global History of Nuclear Disasters.* W.W. Norton and Company, 2023.

Reed, Bruce Cameron. *Manhattan Project: The Story of the Century.* Springer, 2020.

Reed, Bruce Cameron. *The Physics of the Manhattan Project*. Springer, 2021.

Stephens, William E. *Nuclear Fission and Atomic Energy.* Hassell Street Press, 2021.

Tucker, Colin. *How to Drive a Nuclear Reactor.* Springer, 2019.

United Library. *Enrico Fermi: The biography of the father of the nuclear age, physics, and his dedication to the Manhattan Project.* United Library, 2023.

Index

A

B

C

Photo Credits

Front Cover: Shutterstock: D-VISIONS.

Interior: Alamy: Zuma Press 69; **National Geographic:** Albert Moldvay 35; **Public Domain:** American Institute of Physics/Niels Bohr's Nobel Prize Biography 9, Chris McKenna/Thryduulf 62, Simthsonian Institute 14, 38; **Shutterstock:** M Aurelius 6, Liya Blumesser 31, Hung Chung Chih 58, Marcel Clemens 15, D-VISIONS 3, 39, Hywit Dimyadi 68, Eight Photo 50, Everett Historical 16, 25, 45, 46, foto grazia 42, O Guero 10, Nataliya Hora 66, Ihor Khomych 53, Igor Koptyaev 56, Mark Kostich 34, Milosz Maslanka 52, Doug McLean 21, Morphart Creation 13, Nuam folio 64, Mark Oleksiy 61, ricochet64 59, Gabriele Rohde 54, Santiherllor 60, stock 32, Romolo Tavani 70, Dan Thornberg 44, Manoj Kumar Tuteja 7; **United States Government:** United States Department of Energy 18, 19.

T=top, b=bottom, c=center, r=right, l=left, ins=inset.

All other photography and artwork Brown Bear Books.

Brown Bear Books has made every attempt to contact the copyright holder. Please email licensing@brownbearbooks.co.uk if you have any information about omissions.